2004–2005 Annual Supplement to

THE PIANO BOOK

BUYING & OWNING A NEW OR USED PIANO

LARRY FINE

BROOKSIDE PRESS • BOSTON, MASSACHUSETTS

Brookside Press
P.O. Box 178, Jamaica Plain, Massachusetts 02130
(617) 522-7182
(800) 888-4741 (orders: Independent Publishers Group)

info@pianobook.com
www.pianobook.com

Printed in the United States of America

Distributed to the book trade by Independent Publishers Group,
814 North Franklin St., Chicago, IL 60610
(800) 888-4741 or (312) 337-0747

ISBN 1-929145-15-2 (print edition)
ISBN 1-929145-16-0 (electronic edition)

NOTICE

Reasonable efforts have been made to secure accurate information for this publication. Due in part to the fact that manufacturers and distributors will not always willingly make this information available, however, some indirect sources have been relied upon.

Neither the author nor publisher make any guarantees with respect to the accuracy of the information contained herein and will not be liable for damages—incidental, consequential, or otherwise—resulting from the use of the information.

INTRODUCTION

Given the long time span between new editions of *The Piano Book*, it's impractical to provide in the book itself the detailed model and price data that piano shoppers increasingly seek. Similarly, updated information about manufacturers and products is needed in a timely manner. This *Annual Supplement to The Piano Book*, published each summer, is designed to fill that information gap. I hope this modest companion volume will effectively extend the "shelf life" of *The Piano Book* as a valuable reference work, and serve as an additional information resource for piano buyers and piano lovers.

Larry Fine

June, 2004

CONTENTS

MANUFACTURER and PRODUCT UPDATE

This section describes changes to companies, products, and brand names since the fourth edition of *The Piano Book* went to press in the fall of 2000. This section is cumulative; that is, information contained in last year's *Supplement*, to the extent it is still accurate, is repeated here and changes that have occurred during the past year have been added. If a company or brand name is not listed here, it means that there is nothing new of substance to report.

It is not intended, of course, that the information in this update section take the place of the reviews in *The Piano Book*. With some exceptions, the update is limited to changes of a factual nature only, whereas the main book contains, in addition, critical reviews, ratings, and recommendations. Readers should understand that, in most cases, changes in the quality of any particular brand of piano occur very slowly, over a period of many years, if at all. Only where there has been an abrupt change in company ownership, or a period of rapid technological or economic change in the country of origin, is there likely to be a change in quality worth worrying about. For that reason, the reviews in *The Piano Book* can still be considered reliable unless otherwise noted here.

Trends

Pianos made in China continue to improve and make inroads into the North American market. By some estimates, more than one-quarter of all pianos sold in the U.S. in 2003 were made in China. As recently as 2001, most pianos from China, though technically acceptable, were not musically desirable. Over the past couple of years, however, the musical qualities have taken a big leap forward. Though nearly all makes have improved, and most are acceptable, the best vertical pianos are those from the Yantai-Perzina factory, sold here under the Carl Ebel, Perzina, and Gerh. Steinberg labels; the best grands are from the Dongbei factory, sold under the names Nordiska, Everett, Hallet & Davis, and Story & Clark, among others. Pearl River and Ritmüller pianos are also among the better ones. Palatino verticals, brand new this year, also look promising. The jury is still out as to whether these pianos will hold up over the long term and in demanding climates and situations. Anecdotal reports suggest less consistency than with pianos from other countries, but otherwise few major problems. Prices are so low, however, that for many entry-level buyers these pianos are an excellent value despite some uncertainty about their longevity. At least as short-term investments, and in milder climates and less demanding situations, they are probably fine.

(*The Piano Book* contains brand ratings organized by "group," each group representing a level of quality. At the time of publication, I placed most Chinese pianos in Group 5, the lowest level.. At the present time, I would probably place most in Group 4, "Medium quality consumer-grade pianos." Although some actually exhibit the performance characteristics of higher grade instruments, due to their short track record caution would dictate describing them as Group 4 instruments for the time being. See *The Piano Book* for details.)

Although there has been an explosion of different brand names under which Chinese-made pianos are being marketed, there are only about eight Chinese manufacturers that make pianos for export to the U.S. Piano shoppers should keep in mind that, cosmetics aside, if two brands of piano originate in the same factory, they are probably very similar, if not identical.

On the other end of the price spectrum, European piano makers seem to be in a race to redesign their pianos for better sound projection and sustain, à la Steinway. While the European piano market is languishing, the U.S. market for high-end pianos, relatively speaking, is thriving, and for a number of companies, Steinway is the principal competitor. Considering how tradition-bound these companies are, this degree of activity is unusual. Some of the redesigns—new models from Seiler and Schimmel come to mind— have been terrific musical successes. My only worry is that the palette of available piano tonal qualities is becoming smaller and more homogeneous as the old-world sounds pass away.

Changes in China and in Europe, and their far-reaching consequences, are causing a paradigm shift in the piano industry that is making it more difficult to give advice to piano shoppers. A paradigm is a theoretical framework from which generalizations are formulated. For many years, the paradigm for piano quality has been an international pecking order with pianos from Russia and China (and, more recently, Indonesia) at the bottom, followed by Korea, Japan, Eastern Europe, and finally Western Europe (mostly Germany) at the top, with pianos from the United States scattered here and there depending on the brand. While this pecking order has never been foolproof, it has served its purpose as a generalization well enough for use by a generation of piano buyers.

Now these distinctions are being blurred by globalization. Unable to escape the high cost of doing business at home, some Western European manufacturers are developing satellite operations and more affordable second product lines in Eastern Europe. Some makers of high-end instruments are also quietly beginning to source parts and subassemblies from Asia and elsewhere. To the extent they can afford it, they are also investing in high-tech equipment to reduce the expense and inconsistency of hand labor, even while continuing to tout their status as makers of "hand-made" instruments. Some Korean and Chinese manufacturers, on the other hand, are importing parts and technology from Germany and Japan, producing instruments that when well prepared by the dealer rival the performance qualities of far more expensive pianos from Japan and, occasionally, Europe. The most we can say is that their longevity is unknown, an argument that, while true, becomes weaker with each passing year. In addition, global alliances such as that between Samick, Young Chang, and Bechstein (described elsewhere in this *Supplement*) are sure to bring new products to the market that are more hybridized than anything we've seen before. Although the old paradigm still has validity, the number of nonconforming situations is increasing, all of which will cause temporary confusion in the marketplace until such time as a new paradigm emerges.

At the same time that quality differences between low-end and high-end instruments are becoming narrower, price difference are greater than they've ever been, bringing issues of "value" into greater prominence. Eastern European quality in some cases now closely approaches that of Western Europe, but at a price comparable to that of Japan. Some of the better pianos from China and Korea have specifications equal to almost anything from Japan, and workmanship nearly as good, at a fraction of the price. Caught in the middle, the Japanese are gradually being squeezed out of the piano market despite their perennially good quality.

Another consequence of globalization has been the diminishing number of suppliers of parts and materials (actions, hammers, pinblocks, soundboards, keys, plates, etc.) to the piano industry. (Actually, the enormous Chinese piano industry has numerous parts suppliers, but most of these supply parts only for pianos sold in the domestic Chinese market, not internationally.) At one time there were large differences in quality between suppliers, but globalization has reduced and sometimes eliminated those differences. For example, as recently as a few years ago, Detoa (Czech) actions were markedly inferior to Renner actions, and Chinese-made actions were terrible. Now there is at most only a small difference in quality between Detoa and Renner, virtually all Chinese actions are acceptable, and at least one Chinese supplier is said to be on the verge of producing credible knockoffs of Renner actions.

At the same time, many manufacturers continue to use a "recipe" approach to differentiating differently-priced piano lines: Choose an action (Renner, Detoa, Chinese), combine it with a hammer (Renner, Abel, Tokiwa), add a pinblock (Delignit, Dehonit, Bolduc), and so forth, to produce a piano at a particular price. But with fewer suppliers to choose from, and less difference between them, the implied difference in quality at different price points is threatening to become more a matter of image than actuality. Image has always been important in differentiating one piano brand from another, in part because even real differences can be subtle or highly technical and not obvious, especially to those who don't play the instrument well. But with even real differences evaporating, image-spinning is reaching new heights.

The above notwithstanding, differences still do exist. The most important is that between consumer-grade pianos on the one hand (Groups 3, 4, and 5) and performance-grade pianos on the other (Groups 1 and 2). There have been some attempts by makers to bridge this gap (i.e. Knabe by Samick and Shigeru Kawai by Kawai), but for the most part, the two different types of manufacturers still live in two different worlds. The difference between the two worlds is a bit less than it used to be, but it still exists in the form of selection, drying, and use of wood; final regulation and voicing; and attention to technical and cosmetic detail; in other words, the difference is more than just the "recipe." Theoretically, it would not be impossible for, say, a Chinese company to duplicate the finest pianos. But the market for these instruments is small, and some have unique and idiosyncratic designs that are not amenable to mass production. Therefore, it is always likely to be more of a niche market entered into by those whose profit-seeking is mixed with a love for the instrument and perhaps a desire to carry on a family business. At this point in time, such businesses are more likely to be Western than Asian, but who knows . . . that may one day change.

ALTENBURG

Correction to web site address: www.altenburgpiano.com

The F.E. Altenburg line of pianos made by Niendorf is being discontinued.

ASTIN-WEIGHT

Change to web site address: www.astin-weight.com

New e-mail address: gr8pianos@networld.com

BALDWIN

including D.H. Baldwin, Hamilton, Chickering, Wurlitzer, Ellington, ConcertMaster

New address, phone, and ownership:

Baldwin Piano Company
309 Plus Park Blvd.
Nashville, Tennessee 37217

615-871-4500
800-876-2976

Owned by: Baldwin Piano, Inc., a wholly owned subsidiary of Gibson Guitar Corp.

Shortly after the fourth edition of *The Piano Book* was published in early 2001, the Baldwin board of directors hired a new management team to try to stave off impending bankruptcy caused by a series of costly mistakes and prior poor management. Avoiding bankruptcy turned out not to be possible, and the company filed for protection under Chapter 11 of the U.S. bankruptcy laws in May of 2001. On October 16, 2001, Baldwin's major creditor, General Electric Capital, purchased the company's assets at a court-ordered liquidation sale and then sold them to the Gibson Guitar Corp. on November 9, 2001.

Gibson owners Henry Juszkiewicz and Dave Berryman purchased Gibson in 1986 when it was in complete disarray and turned it into an extremely profitable and well-respected company. They feel that there are many parallels between Gibson's situation at that time and Baldwin's present situation, and expect to be able to turn Baldwin around as well.

Baldwin's new owners say they have made large capital investments to improve product quality. In order to make production more efficient, grand production has been moved from Conway, Arkansas and consolidated with vertical production in the company's Trumann, Arkansas facility. A woodworking plant in Greenwood, Mississippi closed in mid-2000 has had its functions transferred to a new woodworking plant in Trumann. The Juarez, Mexico action-making facility has been reopened. Additional cost savings have been realized by the transfer of all Baldwin sales, marketing, and administrative functions to Gibson headquarters in Nashville.

Prior to the management reorganization and subsequent bankruptcy, Baldwin had announced a number of changes to its product line, some of which were reported in *The Piano Book*. These changes were never fully realized due to the bankruptcy. The new owners plan to complete implementation of some of these changes (see comments below), and other changes are to be expected as Baldwin's reorganization evolves.

Baldwin's line of digital pianos has been discontinued.

The Eurostyle consoles and studios (E100, E101, E102, E250, E260) have been discontinued.

In the grands, the new model 225E is the model M (5' 2") in French Provincial styling. Model 227E (model R in Louis XVI styling) has been discontinued. The 7' model SF-10 has been renamed SF-10E in honor of its adoption of the enhanced features of the upgraded Artist series grands (see *The Piano Book* for details).

The Chickering grands reported on in *The Piano Book* have been withdrawn. They were to be replaced by three new models—5' 4", 5' 9", and 6' 2"—made by Samick in Korea, with some cosmetic features taken from old Chickering designs. Due to Baldwin's bankruptcy, however, Baldwin never took possession of these pianos, so they are being sold and warranted by Samick under license from Baldwin while supplies last. In my estimation, the quality should be much better than the Chickerings being withdrawn, probably comparable to other Samick-made instruments.

Also in the grand department, Baldwin has introduced a Custom Grand Finishes program, allowing customers to design their own grand piano. Four levels of customization are available: 1) wood-finish accents on regular grands; 2) colors (Jubilee Red, Golden Honey, Evergreen, Beale Street Blue, Madeira); 3) exotic wood veneers; and 4) anything you want. A Custom Vertical program includes the limited edition Gibson studio, each one signed by guitarist Les Paul, and the Elvis Presley Signature model, authorized by the Presley estate.

Baldwin has developed, and is now including, its new "Stealth"™ action in all 43" and 45" Baldwin vertical pianos. The "Full Blow" action, in use since 1939, has been updated with a Schwander-style hammer-butt return spring and other changes for improved quietness, responsiveness, durability, and ease of servicing. You can recognize the Stealth™ action by its visually striking deep blue color. In addition, vertical pianos with the new action have model numbers ending in "E."

Baldwin has introduced several new lower-cost lines of piano. Only briefly introduced in 2003 and then discontinued was the Ellington brand name. This is a name originally produced by Baldwin from 1893 to 1930 as its lower-priced alternative to the Baldwin line. The most recent Ellingtons were made in China, verticals by the Beijing Piano Co. (see "Beijing") and grands by Sejung (see "Sejung").

The Ellington line has been replaced by the "Hamilton." Not to be confused with the famous Hamilton model studio piano Baldwin has made for decades with "Baldwin" on the fallboard, these new Hamiltons say "Hamilton" on the fallboard. Currently they are made in China by Sejung. The verticals are available in both continental and American furniture styles, have a solid spruce soundboard, and come with a ten-year parts and labor warranty. A 73-note spinet is part of this line. The company says that except for the number of notes, this is a true acoustic piano with all the features of a full-size piano. The grands, 4' 7", 5' 1", and 5' 8", feature solid spruce soundboards and a ten-year parts and labor warranty.

Another new line is the D.H. Baldwin. Those in the piano trade may recall this as a name Baldwin used on a line of pianos made in Korea. The new D.H. Baldwin line, however, is made in Arkansas. The 560 and 570 model verticals are based on the Acrosonic scale, the model 4560 on the Baldwin model 243 studio scale, and the model M5 on the Baldwin M1 grand scale. The company says these new models are essentially like their higher-priced cousins musically, but with scaled-down cabinetry. Also made in Arkansas are pianos with a variety of minor brand names Baldwin owns and uses at dealer request, such as Ivers & Pond, Cable, J & C Fischer, and others. These are essentially the same as the D.H. Baldwin pianos.

As for Baldwin's Wurlitzer line of pianos, the verticals have been discontinued and the grands are now made by Samick in Korea. They come in two levels of quality, "C" and "WP." The "WP" models have a slow-close fallboard and upgraded cabinetry and cosmetics.

When Gibson acquired Baldwin, it acquired only its assets, not its liabilities. Therefore, the company is not required to honor warranty claims for pianos purchased prior to the acquisition date. Pianos purchased by the consumer from an authorized dealer on or after November 9, 2001 are eligible for warranty coverage, even if the dealer purchased the piano before that date. Warranty coverage for pianos purchased by the consumer before November 9, 2001 will only be considered on a case-by-case basis.

In mid-April 2002, Baldwin cancelled agreements with most of its dealers, retaining only the most active ones. Since then the company has been steadily rebuilding its dealer network, inviting new dealers to demonstrate their commitment, in part by making large purchases from the company. Baldwin says, however, that it *will* honor the warranty on pianos purchased from "cancelled" dealers, even though, technically, they are no longer "authorized" dealers.

Gibson appears to have a reasonable chance to turn Baldwin around. The company also has a good track record with regard to continued ownership of other acquired companies and the honoring of their warranties. Nevertheless, such undertakings are obviously not without risk. Therefore, I would advise purchasers of Baldwin products to obtain a written warranty from the dealer covering parts and labor for at least ten years in addition to whatever manufacturer's warranty may come with the product.

BECHSTEIN, C.

New North American distributor:

SMC (formerly Samick Music Corp.)
18521 Railroad Street
City of Industry, California 91748

626-964-4700
800-592-9393
www.bechstein.de

Korean piano maker Samick has purchased a majority interest in C. Bechstein by acquiring the shares held by Karl Schulze, Bechstein's largest shareholder. Schulze also purchased a fifteen percent interest in Samick. Samick will help Bechstein increase production, diversify its product line, and sell in North America, and Bechstein will help Samick improve technically and market its pianos in Europe. Bechstein will remain as a separately managed German corporation.

Bechstein has introduced a new series of very beautiful designer verticals called "ProBechstein" in 45½", 46½", and 49" sizes. In the Pricing Guide section, they are the models called "Balance," "Avance," and "Ars Nova."

The 9' 2" model D-280 concert grand has been redesigned, with a capo bar and duplex scale in the treble for better tonal projection and tonal color. Also, unlike most other Bechsteins, which utilize an open pinblock design, this concert grand plate covers the pinblock area. These features have also been added to the new 6' 4" model M/P-192 grand and the 6' 11" B-210. The 7' 6" C-232 remains unchanged for the time being.

SMC, Samick's North American distribution arm, will market and distribute Bechstein pianos in the U.S. and Canada. The verticals and grands mentioned above, plus the 51½" Concert 8 vertical, will be called the

"Concert Series" and will say "C. Bechstein" on the fallboard. This line will use the best quality materials and receive the best voicing. The older, unenhanced versions of the above grands, namely models 160 (5' 3"), 190 (6' 3"), and 208 (6' 10"), plus models 180 (5' 9") and 208 (6' 9") to be released during 2004 and 2005, will be known as the "Academy Series" and will say only "Bechstein" on the fallboard. The company says that materials for this lower-priced line will be "sourced worldwide for value."

The W. Hoffmann line of pianos has been discontinued in the U.S. and Canada. A version of this piano from the same factory (Bohemia) will continue to be sold here under the "Bohemia" name by the Bohemia Piano Co. (see "Bohemia").

BECKER, J.

Distribution of these pianos in the U.S. has been discontinued.

BEHNING

Distribution discontinued. See "Weber"

BEIJING XINGHAI

Beijing Piano Factory, part of the Beijing Xinghai Musical Instruments Co., has been producing pianos since 1949 and manufactures more than fifty thousand vertical and grand pianos annually. They are available throughout the world under the Otto Meister and Xinghai labels, as well as under various other labels as joint ventures with other manufacturers and distributors, including Heintzmann (in Canada), Ellington (Baldwin), Story & Clark, and Wyman. Kawai also has a joint venture with Beijing, though the pianos are distributed only in Canada and Europe, not the U.S. (at one time they bore the name "Linden").

The assets of Canadian piano manufacturer Heintzman were purchased by a Chinese company and moved from Canada to Beijing, where pianos are now produced under the Heintzman name in joint venture with the Beijing Piano Factory by a firm known as Beijing Heintzman. Prices were not available at press time. Although information about these pianos is scarce, my sources tell me that the quality is a little higher than that of some of the other Beijing-made pianos.

BERGMANN

See "Young Chang"

BLONDEL, G.

Distribution of Blondel pianos in the U.S. has been discontinued.

BLÜTHNER

In honor of the company's 150th anniversary, Blüthner has introduced a Jubilee model which has a commemorative cast-iron plate in the style of the special-edition pianos of a century ago. Any grand piano model can be special-ordered with this commemorative plate.

In what is perhaps a world's "first," Blüthner has designed and built a piano for left-handed pianists. This is a completely "backwards" piano, with the treble keys, hammers, and strings on the left and the bass on the right. When it was introduced, a pianist gave a concert on it after only a couple of hours of practice! It is currently available in the 6' 10" and 9' 2" sizes by special order (price not available).

BOHEMIA (new listing)

German American Trading, Inc.
P.O. Box 17789
Tampa, Florida 33682

813-961-8405
germanamer@aol.com

Pianos made by: Bohemia Piano Co., Hradec Kralove, Czech Republic.

The factory that makes Bohemia pianos began production in 1871, after World War II becoming part of the Czech state-owned enterprise that included the better-known Petrof. Privatized in 1993, Bohemia now makes 2,000 verticals and 300 grands per year. Originally it exported to the U.S. under the name Rieger-Kloss (now discontinued). The name Bohemia is derived from the original term used by the ancient Romans for the part of Europe that is now the Czech Republic.

Specifications for the instruments include Czech solid spruce soundboards, Czech-made sand-cast plates, either Czech Detoa actions on Bohemia action frames or Renner parts on Bohemia action frames (the latter denoted by

"BR" in model numbers), either Renner or Abel hammers, and either Detoa or Kluge keyboards. All pianos come with a leather upholstered adjustable artist bench, and the grands all have slow-close fallboards.

The Bohemia grands I played at a trade show sounded and felt very good, with a nice, bright, singing treble tone.

Warranty: Ten years, parts and labor.

BÖSENDORFER

New U.S. distributor address, phone, and e-mail:

Bösendorfer Representing Office
1618 West Catalpa, 1st floor
Chicago, Illinois 60640

888-936-2516
bosendorferusa@aol.com

In January 2002, Bösendorfer was purchased from Kimball International by the BAWAG - P.S.K. Group, Austria's third largest banking group. Bösendorfer has a special place in Austrian history and culture, and although the company has thrived under Kimball's ownership, for some time there has been a desire on all sides to return Bösendorfer to Austrian hands. The new owner says it intends to maintain the same high standards of material and workmanship for which the company is renowned. It will also continue the new marketing course of the last few years, including the redesign of existing models, a new "Artisan" series of art case pianos, and the Conservatory series of cosmetically reduced, less expensive versions of its models.

In 2001, Bösendorfer introduced a new 9' 2" model 280 concert grand, and in 2002, a 6' 1" model 185 grand. These and other new and redesigned models share a new design philosophy in which the treble soundboard area is increased for better tonal projection by reducing excess cabinet distance between player and strings, and the bass soundboard area is increased for better bass response by joining the wide tail to the spine at a sharper corner. Action geometry has been improved, the company says, on all models.

The new concert grand is in addition to the two other concert grands (9' and 9' 6") the company already produces. Unlike the others, however, which have 92 and 97 keys, respectively, this new model has only 88 keys. Its scale design also features a front duplex. The company says the new model is intended for concert pianists who would otherwise be distracted or intimidated by the presence of additional keys in the bass. To my ears, the new piano has better sustain in the treble than I usually find in Bösendorfer pianos, but otherwise has a characteristic Bösendorfer sound and feel. The 9' model 275 is now available only by special order.

Bösendorfer showed several new models in 2003: a Porsche-designed modern piano suggestive of an automobile, a Victorian-styled piano called "Vienna," and two 175th anniversary models limited to a production run of 175 instruments each. The anniversary models, 52" model 130 and 5' 8" model 175, have such cosmetic enhancements as a burl walnut fallboard, gold trim, and a numbered medallion. Aside from the cosmetic enhancements, model 175 is the equivalent of a model 170 in the Conservatory series (not normally offered in this size), except with a high polish finish instead of satin. In 2004, the Anniversary models were retired. The Conservatory series models described in *The Piano Book* are now limited to models 200 and 214.

The SE Reproducer system, out of production for a number of years, is being brought back in 2005 with updated electronics and solenoids. Bösendorfer says that the library for it will have top performers and that the system will play other disc formats as well.

BOSTON

The 49" vertical model UP-125 has been replaced with a completely redesigned 50" model UP-126. In the redesign, the wooden back has been made much heftier and the plate much more rigid to better resist torsional and bending stresses. Similar changes have also been made to the 52" model UP-132E, and the 46" model UP-118E. In the two larger models, the bass scale has been reworked with reduced string tension for smoother bass tone, and the soundboard taper and rib placement have been refined for better treble tone. Lastly, the music desk for the European-style case design has been improved so that it holds music more securely. Boston says it has plans to redesign the grands over time using the same structural analysis software employed in the design of its Essex line of pianos.

BREITMANN (new listing)

German Piano Imports LLC
5660 W. Grand River Ave.
Lansing, Michigan 48906

517-886-6000
800-954-3200

info@bluthnerpiano.com
www.bluthnerpiano.com

Pianos made by: Artfield Piano Ltd., Qing Pu, China

Breitmann is a brand associated with Blüthner and made in China. Features include Delignit pinblocks, laminated spruce soundboards, German strings, Japanese hammers, and Renner parts in the grands.

THE BRITISH PIANO MANUFACTURING COMPANY LTD. (new listing)

This was, for a time, the new name for the company formerly known as Whelpdale, Maxwell & Codd. This company produced Welmar, Knight, Broadwood, Bentley, and Woodchester pianos. It purchased Woodchester in 2001 and moved the manufacturing facilities for all its brands to the Woodchester factory, formerly the Bentley factory (see *The Piano Book* for history).

In April, 2003, this company ceased operations. Its assets were purchased by a piano distributor in the United Kingdom, who said he has no immediate plans to reissue the brand names.

Clarification: In *The Piano Book* entry for Whelpdale Maxwell & Codd, I wrote that John Broadwood & Sons was established in 1728. It has been brought to my attention that this is not possible because Broadwood was not born until 1732. The 1728 (or 1729) date is widely used, however, and it probably represents the date of establishment of the shop of Burkat Shudi, with whom Broadwood apprenticed (1761), and of whose business Broadwood later became partner (1770) and, eventually, sole proprietor (1782).

CHASE, A. B. (new listing)

Musical Properties, Inc.
949 French Drive
Mundelein, Illinois 60060

773-342-4212

Pianos made by: Dongbei Piano Co., Dongbei, China

A. B. Chase is an old American piano name, formerly owned by Aeolian Pianos but to the best of my knowledge not used since that company's bankruptcy in 1985. Since 2001, the brand has been used by Musical Properties, Inc. on pianos from the Dongbei piano factory in China.

CHICKERING

See "Baldwin"

CABLE, HOBART M.

See "Sejung"

DISKLAVIER

See "Yamaha"

EBEL, CARL

See "Perzina, Gebr."

EISENBERG

See "Steinberg, Wilh."

ELLINGTON

See "Baldwin"

ESSEX

Steinway, through its Boston Piano Co. subsidiary, introduced several "Essex" models in early 2001 and 2002. These are manufactured in Korea by Young Chang. They include 5' 3" and 6' grands and 42" and 44" verticals. The vertical models are of identical scale design, but the smaller one is in a continental-style cabinet. Some of the vertical cabinets look backward to styles of past decades of the twentieth century. The grands are available in both traditional and Art Deco styles, the difference being in the styling of the music desk, and in a Chippendale style.

Steinway says that it designed these pianos using state-of-the-art structural analysis software similar to that used in the auto and aircraft industries, allowing it to test the effects of a large number of variables in a short amount of time without having to build innumerable prototypes. Like Boston pianos, the Essex line was designed with a lower tension duplex scale and a larger, tapered solid spruce soundboard, for potentially better sustain. The grands utilize rosette-shaped flanges for better action stability.

ESTONIA

In 2001, having purchased the remaining shares in the company from the company employees, the former majority owner became the sole owner of the company. The name of the company has been changed to reflect his ownership.

New U.S. distributor contact information:

Laul Estonia Piano Factory
7 Fillmore Drive
Stony Point, New York 10980

845-947-7763
laulestoniapiano@aol.com
www.laulestoniapiano.com

The company reports that it has made a large number of changes and improvements during the past three years, among which are: rescaling the bass and upgrading bass string making machinery; improving the method of drilling pinblocks; stronger plates and improved plate finishes; thicker inner rims on the 5' 6" grands; improved fitting of soundboard to rim; concert-grand-quality soundboard spruce on all models; quarter-sawn maple bridge caps; an adjustable duplex scale; wood for legs and keyslips treated to better resist moisture; Renner Blue hammers on all models; better quality metal hardware that resists oxidation; suede-covered music desk tray; improved satin finishes; establishing a quality control department headed by the elder Mr. Laul (both he and his wife are professional musicians); higher-grade and better-prepared veneers; and establishing a U.S. service center for warranty repairs. All pianos are now accompanied by a quality control certificate signed by a member of the Laul family.

Concerning the criticisms in *The Piano Book*, technicians report that Estonia pianos are now arriving at the dealer well-prepared, and seem not to have problems anymore with uneven tuning pin tightness. Based on technical improvements the company has made and new information from technicians, I would raise both the "Confidence" and "Quality Control" ratings of Estonia pianos to four and a half stars (see *The Piano Book* for details about the rating system).

ETERNA

Distribution discontinued.

EVERETT

New distributor phone number: 800-336-9164

Most Everett models are made by the Dongbei Piano Co. in Dongbei, China. However, the EV-111 furniture-style consoles and the EV-174 5' 8" grand are made by a different Chinese company, one that calls itself "Everett" and manufactures pianos under the Everett name for the domestic Chinese market.

FALCONE

See "Sejung"

FAZIOLI

Corrections to review: Three lids are optional on the 10' 2" grand. The 5' 2", 6', and 6' 11" models utilize a Delignit pinblock as mentioned, but the larger models have Bolduc (Canadian) pinblocks. The Fazioli warranty has been increased to ten years.

Additional web site address: www.fazioli.com

FEURICH

New U.S. representative:

Unique Pianos, Inc.
159 Parkhill Blvd.
Melbourne, Florida 32904

888-725-6633
321-725-5690
www.feurich.com

Pianos made by: Feurich Klavier-u.Flügelfabrikation GmbH, Gunzenhausen, Germany

This venerable German manufacturer is once again making pianos in its own factory. The models being offered at this time are 5' 8" (F172) and 7' 5" (F227) grands and a 49" (F123) vertical.

FÖRSTER, AUGUST

New web site address: www.august-foerster.de

GROTRIAN

Grotrian now distributes directly from the factory:

Grotrian Piano Company
P.O. Box 5833
D-38049 Braunschweig, Germany

49-531-210100
49-531-2101040 (fax)
contact@grotrian.de
www.grotrian.de

The "Friedrich Grotrian" is a new 44" vertical with a beech back frame but no back posts, and a simpler cabinet, at a lower price than regular Grotrian pianos.

Grotrian has introduced the Duo Grand Piano, two grand pianos placed side by side with keyboards at opposite ends, as in a duo piano concert, with removable rim parts, connected soundboards, and a common lid (price not available).

HALLET, DAVIS & CO.

Many of the Chinese-made Hallet & Davis pianos are now being made by the Dongbei Piano Co.

HAYDEN (new listing)

American Piano Distributors, Inc.
P.O. Box 21472
Roanoke, Virginia 24018

540-776-7900
888-MUSIC-12
Haydenmusic@aol.com
www.HaydenPiano.us

Pianos made by: Dongbei Piano Co., Dongbei, China

While Hayden pianos are currently manufactured by the Dongbei Piano Co., the distributor says it eventually plans to offer models from a number of different factories and countries.

HAZELTON BROS.

See "Samick"

HEINTZMAN

See "Beijing Xinghai"

HOFFMANN, W.

Bechstein has discontinued distribution of W. Hoffmann pianos in North America. Most of these instruments were manufactured by the Bohemia Piano Co. in the Czech Republic. Similar instruments are now being marketed in the U.S. under the Bohemia name by the manufacturer. See "Bohemia."

IBACH

New U.S. distributor information:

Resource West, Inc.
2295 E. Sahara Avenue
Las Vegas, Nevada 89104

702-457-7919
800-777-6874
info@ibachpiano.com
www.ibachpiano.com

The real German Ibach pianos are once again being distributed in the United States. Resource West says it will be distributing these fine pianos through interior design professionals and some smaller piano dealers. No investment is needed by the dealer. In lieu of stocking the pianos and receiving a regular retail markup, the dealer instead refers interested customers to the Resource West/Ibach showroom in Las Vegas and receives a substantial commission when a sale is made. Resource West prepares the pianos and delivers them to the customers. The price list in this *Supplement* is the suggested retail price at the Las Vegas showroom.

The Ibach-Daewoo joint venture mentioned in *The Piano Book* was discontinued and the Korean manufacturing operation was sold by Daewoo to an investment group that continued to manufacture pianos in Korea on a limited basis. These pianos were distributed for a time in the U.S. under the name Bachendorff (an arrangement now discontinued) and in Canada under the name Royale. At press time, a distributor operating under the name

Persis International, Inc. says it will be having this Korean company make pianos under the Sohmer name (see "Sohmer").

IRMLER

The Chinese-made Irmlers have been discontinued. The European Irmlers are made in Poland with the technological assistance of Blüthner. Final action assembly and regulation is performed in the Blüthner factory in Germany.

KAWAI

Additional web site address: www.shigerukawai.com

Kawai has opened a factory in Indonesia, where it will be making some piano models sold in the U.S., as well as cabinets and back assemblies for some models to be assembled in its North Carolina facility. Over the next year, Kawai plans to move all its U.S. manufacturing to Indonesia and close the North Carolina plant. Kawai also produces several vertical models in joint venture with the Beijing Xinghai Piano Co. in China. These pianos are known as the KX models, and are sold in Canada and Europe, but not in the U.S. At one time these pianos bore the name "Linden," but use of that name has been discontinued.

True to its reputation, Kawai has made even more changes to its product line. The model 505 and 605 furniture-style consoles have been discontinued and replaced with several 44½" and 45" models utilizing the same scale design as the 605. Model 506 is this piano in a simple, studio-style cabinet, made in Indonesia. Although called a "studio" because of the cabinet style, it has a compressed action characteristic of a console. Model 508 is the same as the 506, except with a fancier cabinet and assembled in North Carolina with an Indonesian back. Model 606 is the Indonesian-made model as a furniture-style console; model 608 is the 606 with a fancier cabinet containing inlaid veneers, assembled in North Carolina with an Indonesian back.

Among the Japanese-made models, model K-18 is the 506 in a Japanese-style, polyester-finished cabinet. It replaces the recent CX-10 and its predecessor, the popular model CX-5H, as Kawai's low-priced "studio." The 46½" furniture-style studio model 902 has been changed to model 906, with a stiffer back structure, all ABS action parts, and new cabinetry. Model K-25 is like the 48" model K-30 (discontinued), except in a simpler cabinet. UST-10 and UST-12 are, respectively, 48" and 52" American-style institutional (school) uprights, similar internally to the K-25 and K-60 uprights.

Kawai has invented a variable-touch action for vertical pianos in which the player can vary the touchweight by sliding a lever. The lever operates a set of sliding weights behind the fallboard. The touchweight varies depending on the point at which the keys contact the sliding weights. The touchweight can be adjusted from 48 to 70 grams (normal for Kawai is 56 grams). The "Vari-Touch" feature is currently available on the 46" UST-8 studio (model VT-118) and on the 52" K-60 upright (model VT-132).

In the grands, the 5' model GM-2A has become model GM-10, which is further divided into two levels of cabinetry. The GM-10C is the original GM-10, with a non-movable music desk (a nuisance) and a plain cabinet. The GM-10LE is an upgraded version, with a movable music desk and a nicer cabinet. The 5' 1" model GE-1A has been replaced by the GE-20, which has the features of the former GE-1AS model. A new 5' 5" model GE-30 has been introduced. It has the same scale as the model RX-1, but is like the other GE models structurally and in terms of its features (see *The Piano Book* for details on the differences between the RX, GE, and GM models).

As explained in *The Piano Book*, Kawai uses ABS Styran plastic as the material for many of its action parts. In 2004, the company introduced a new generation of these parts, made of ABS Styran mixed with carbon fibers. The carbon fibers allow the parts to be more rigid with less weight and to be more finely engineered for shape and texture, resulting in a faster, lighter action and more consistent touch. I played two pianos of identical model, one with the older parts and one with the new, and could sense a substantial difference. At present, the new parts are found in the RX and Shigeru Kawai grands.

Several of the grand and upright models are available in limited quantity in "Conservatory" and "Promotional" versions. The Conservatory model uprights have a wider music rack than the regular models, usually larger or double casters and a lock, and sometimes cabinetry or aesthetics that are slightly simplified. Promotional models have a regular (not soft-fall) fallboard and some other simplified features. Prices were not available at press time, but are expected to be about the same or slightly less than regular models.

Kawai's high-end Shigeru Kawai line of pianos is now available in six different models from 5' 10" to 9' 1".

KEMBLE

Kemble is now acting as its own distributor for most of the U.S. The factory contact information is:

Kemble & Company Ltd.
Mount Avenue
Bletchley, Milton Keynes MK1 1JE
United Kingdom

44-1908-371771
44-1908-270448 (fax)
brian_kemble@gmx.yamaha.com
www.kemble-pianos.co.uk

In the southern U.S., contact: Unique Pianos, 159 Parkhill Blvd., Melbourne, Florida 32904; phone (888) 725-6633.

A new 46½" "Windsor" model has been added to the Kemble line. This model has a fancier cabinet and a more powerful bass than the 45" "Traditional" model, discontinued. The 52" model K131 vertical, formerly available only as a limited-edition designer model, is now available as a regular model. There is also a new 48" Shaker-styled designer upright called "Vermont" designed by the famous British designers Conran and Partners, a 45" black polyester and chrome model called "Classic-T," and a 49" model called "Quantum II" with a sound-escape mechanism.

Kemble has introduced its first grand piano, a 5' 8" "Conservatoire" model, in cooperation with Yamaha, which owns a majority interest in Kemble. The grand is like the Yamaha model C2, with design differences such as plate color and music desk shape. It is also voiced to Kemble's specs, sounding to me more "European," i.e. a mellower bass.

KINGSBURG

This brand is now called Carl Ebel. See under "Perzina, Gebr."

KLIMA (new listing)

Poppenberg & Associates
966 South Pearl Street
Denver, Colorado 80209

303-765-5775
pianopop@ix.netcom.com
www.klima-piano.cz

Pianos made by: Klima-Piano Manufacture s.r.o, Hradec Králové, Czech Republic

Klima is a small Czech piano manufacturer established in 1991 when the state-run piano manufacturing apparatus was sold off to several private firms, including Petrof. Several generations of the Klima family had been Petrof employees. Klima makes about four hundred vertical pianos a year in three models. One model of grand piano is available by special order only. The pianos utilize Czech Detoa actions, but Renner actions are available.

Klima vertical pianos are also available under the Fandrich & Sons label with a Fandrich vertical action installed. See *The Piano Book* for details and contact information.

KNABE, WM.

The Wm. Knabe piano line made by Young Chang for PianoDisc has been discontinued, and PianoDisc has licensed the name to Samick. Samick is now using this name on the pianos formerly sold as the "World Piano" premium line of Samick pianos (see *The Piano Book* for details). Gradually the grands are being redesigned, the new models based on the original nineteenth and early twentieth century Knabe scale designs and cabinet styles in use when the company was based in Baltimore, with sand-cast plates, lacquer finishes, Renner actions and hammers, maple and oak rim, and other high quality features. At present, this redesign has resulted in the 5' 8" (WKG-58) and 6' 4" (WKG-64), with the other grand models still based on the World Piano series. The pianos are serviced in Samick's Los Angeles facility before being shipped to dealers.

I have watched the Knabe line develop over the last couple of years and have noted many improvements. The ones I played at the most recent trade show were still a work in progress, but impressive, especially for a Korean piano. In preparation for this *Supplement*, I also made inquiry among my sources around the country. The pianos arrive in very good condition cosmetically. Most are also well-prepared technically, though not always. In a few cases, technicians found it necessary to completely re-weight the keyboard after correctly regulating the action. A few pianos in bone-dry regions have experienced structural and mechanical problems in the winter, including cracked soundboards. The dealers diligently repaired or replaced the affected pianos, and Samick responded by switching soundboard suppliers to avoid further problems. Other parts of the country did not report problems. When well prepared, most observers thought the pianos to be very musical, well-designed, and a good value. For the time being, I would recommend paying special attention to humidity control in dry climates.

KRAKAUER

New e-mail address: daguillaume@earthlink.net

Change of phone number: 574-262-9952

Krakauer now makes two models of grand piano, with a Korean-made action and Abel hammers.

MASON & HAMLIN

In 2004, Mason & Hamlin reintroduced its 6' 4" model AA grand piano, a model the company manufactured during the first half of the twentieth century. The current version is modified somewhat from the old, but does have features typical of the company's other models, such as a wide tail, a full-perimeter plate, and the patented "tension resonator" crown retention system. In the process of developing the model, the company says, it standardized certain features, refined manufacturing processes, and modernized jigs and machinery, improvements that will now be applied to the other models the company makes. I played a prototype of the AA at a trade show and think it has the potential for becoming the company's most popular model.

McPHAIL (new listing)

McPhail Piano Ltd.
796 Boston Post Road
Marlboro, Massachusetts 01752

866-MCPHAIL (627-4245)
www.auditionapiano.com

Pianos made by: Sejung Corp., Quingdao, China

McPhail is the name of an old Boston-based piano manufacturer from the late eighteenth and early nineteenth centuries. The current McPhail Piano Ltd. was founded in the Boston area in 2003. Pianos are available on a rent to own basis and are marketed through "partners" — music stores, piano teachers, and schools — but not through regular piano dealerships. The "Audition Program" was developed to offer beginners a new instrument with proper touch and tone, but with low investment risk, as an alternative to a used piano or electric keyboard.

Customers "audition" (rent) a McPhail piano for six months, after which they may return the instrument or purchase it with all rent payments credited toward the purchase price. The company arranges all preparation, delivery, and contractual matters.

Presently, McPhail offers 44" consoles and 47" studios in various cabinet designs and 5' and 5' 4" grands. Monthly rental charges range from $75 to $95 for verticals and $175 to $225 for grands. All McPhail pianos feature solid spruce soundboards, sand-cast plates, and maple action parts and come with a twelve-year parts/ten-year labor warranty. The pianos are currently manufactured by Sejung in China.

MEISTER, OTTO

See "Beijing Xinghai"

MILLER, HENRY F. (new listing)

Henry F. Miller
236 West Portal Ave. #568
San Francisco, California 94127

info@henryfmiller.com

This is the name of an old American piano maker dating back to 1863, no longer in business. The name is now owned by the Sherman Clay chain of piano stores. Current Henry F. Miller pianos are made by Pearl River in China and are similar to pianos sold under the Pearl River name. However, the company says in the future it may source these pianos from a variety of Asian manufacturers. The pianos are sold in Sherman Clay, Jordan Kitt's, and other major piano retailers throughout the country.

NORDISKA

Several new models include: a 43" model 109 continental-style console, a 48" model 118 console-styled upright, a 50" model 126 upright with six full-length spruce backposts, among other features; and 7' and 9' grands with maple rims and Renner actions. All the verticals except model 109 have Abel hammers. The 7' grand has an especially good sound and touch, the best yet on a Chinese-made piano.

PALATINO (new listing)

Palatino Piano
5538 Shirley Lane
Montclair, California 91763

909-626-1803
piano@palatinousa.com
www.axlusa.com

Pianos made by: AXL Musical Instruments Co., Ltd. Corp., Shanghai, China

Although this company is new to the piano world, it is not new to music. For some time, AXL has been manufacturing a full range of musical instruments under its own name and under OEM agreements with other companies.

At present the company makes three models of vertical piano. Grands are expected to follow shortly. Specifications include solid spruce soundboard, hard rock maple pinblock and bridges, adjustable artist bench with all models, and a ten-year full warranty. The company says that its factory is very automated, employing CNC routers from Japan and Germany, and that it sources materials for the pianos from around the world. Several verticals I inspected at a trade show were definitely better than the average piano from China and had apparently arrived in excellent condition, needing hardly any preparation. It seems this was not an isolated case, as other people are starting to report similar observations. This is a brand to watch.

PEARL RIVER

New contact information for U.S. distributor:

Pearl River Piano Group America, Ltd.
2260 S. Haven Avenue, Suite F
Ontario, California 91761

909-673-9155
800-435-5086
usa@pearlriverpiano.com
www.pearlriverpiano.com

Pearl River has added 5' 7" and 6' 4" grands to its line. The company says these models are scaled to sound like Japanese or American pianos, whereas the other models are more European sounding. The 7' and 9' Pearl River grands now come with Renner actions. Actions for all other models are made by Pearl River.

A 49" vertical model 126R has been added to the Ritmüller line. The vertical is based on the model 125M1 joint venture piano (with Yamaha), but with agraffes throughout the scale. Renner action is standard on the 7' Ritmüller grand, and available at additional cost on the smaller models.

PERZINA, GEBR. (new listing)

Piano Empire, Inc.
13370 E. Firestone Blvd., Ste. A
Santa Fe Springs, California 90670

800-576-3463
562-926-1906
info@perzinapianos.com
www.perzinapianos.com

Pianos made by: Yantai-Perzina Piano Manufacturing Co., Ltd., Yantai, China. Some names formerly made by Yantai Longfeng Piano Co.

Names used: Gebr. Perzina, Carl Ebel, Gerh. Steinberg.

Name formerly used: Kingsburg

The Gebr. Perzina piano company was established in the German town of Schwerin in 1871, and was a prominent piano maker until World War I, after which its fortunes declined. In more recent times, the factory was moved to the nearby city of Lenzen and the company is now known as Pianofabrik Lenzen GmbH. In the early 1990s, the company was purchased by Music Brokers International B.V. in The Netherlands. Eventually it was decided that making pianos in Germany was not economically viable, so manufacturing was moved to Yantai, China, where a range of verticals and grands were made for a number of years by the Yantai Longfeng Piano Co. under the Perzina name. The Kingsburg name was also used. (See also under "Kingsburg" in *The Piano Book*.) In 2003, Music Brokers International established its own factory in Yantai, called Yantai-Perzina Piano Manufacturing Co. Ltd., where it now builds the Perzina, Carl Ebel, and Gerh. Steinberg pianos. (Note: Do not confuse Gerh. Steinberg with Wilh. Steinberg, a German piano brand.)

The three brand names are all based on the same scale designs, but there are technical and cosmetic differences between them, with the Perzina brand positioned as highest quality, followed by the Steinberg and the Carl Ebel.

The technical differences revolve primarily around the choice of action, hammers, and soundboard design, among other things. In particular, the Perzina brand is distinguished by use of a Bavarian white spruce (instead of Sitka spruce) tapered soundboard. In addition, the Perzina verticals have several interesting features rarely found in other pianos, including a "floating" soundboard that is unattached to the back at certain points for freer vibration, and a reverse, or concave, soundboard crown. The Perzina grands are available with either Detoa or Renner action. The company says that the Perzina pianos also receive a higher level of attention to detail at the end of the manufacturing process.

The company's European headquarters says it ships many European materials to Yantai, including Roslau strings, Delignit pinblocks, Abel hammers, English felts, European veneers, and Bavarian white spruce soundboards. New machinery is from Germany, Japan and Italy. According to the company, all the piano designs are the original German scales. The Renner actions used in some of the Perzina grands are ordered complete from Germany, not assembled from parts.

PETROF

Web site address: www.petrof.com

Petrof has introduced a new concert grand called the "P1 Mistral." The company says the instrument utilizes a more rigid brace and frame, front and rear duplex scales, and a Renner action, among other features. The Magnetic Balanced Action feature (see page 233 of *The Piano Book*) is available as an option. Also new is a 53" vertical model P135. It has a Renner action, full sostenuto, a soft-close fallboard, and a newly-designed adjustable music desk, among other features. Several of the vertical models are now available with designer panels with inlays.

All Petrof grands are now being shipped with Abel hammers. They should be easier to voice than the harder hammers previously used. Consequently, piano shoppers are now more likely to find individual Petrof grands with a mellower tone.

PIANODISC

PianoDisc has replaced the PDS 128 Plus system with the 228 CFX. The main difference is that the 228 CFX has both a floppy drive and a CD drive as standard equipment, so it is unnecessary to plug in your own CD player (although you can do so if you have a multi-disc CD changer you want to use). The company says that the control box is the smallest such box with both floppy and CD drives on the market. It can be mounted on the piano or can be located up to 100 feet away and operated with the included infrared wireless remote control.

PianoDisc has introduced an MX Platinum option that utilizes 64 MB of flash memory to store hours of music and play it back without ever having to change a disk. MX Platinum comes with 35 hours of pre-selected music (589 songs), to which one can add music from floppy disks, TFT MIDI Record, and standard MIDI files (but not PianoDisc CDs). PianoDisc's regular MX feature with 32 MB of flash memory still remains available as an option.

The GT360 and GT90 QuietTime systems have been discontinued and replaced with a QuietTime system that includes most of the same components, but without the sound card and control box. The new system comes with a power supply, MIDI cable, a MIDI strip for installing under the keys, three pedal switches, a MIDI board with cover, headphones, and a mute rail that, when activated, prevents the hammers from hitting the strings. Customers can buy and use any off-the-shelf sound module with the system.

A question often arises concerning the relationship of the PianoDisc system components to the QuietTime system. The answer is that if you purchase the PianoDisc playback system with the SymphonyPro Sound Module, the TFT MIDI Record system, and the PianoMute Rail, you have purchased virtually all the components of the QuietTime system and have therefore acquired the QuietTime system virtually "free." The separate listing for QuietTime in the price list is for those who wish to purchase it without the PianoDisc playback. Those people will need to purchase, in addition, a sound module from their music dealer.

PianoDisc has introduced a new remote control called the PianoDisc Home Theater Master. It features an LCD touch screen and eliminates the need to have multiple remote controls to operate other various electronic devices. This remote is specially programmed to operate the PianoDisc and can be programmed to control eleven other Audio and Video components including: Stereo, CD, Tape, CATV, Satellite, TV, DVD, VCR and Laser Disc.

Note Release Control (NRC) has been developed by PianoDisc to reduce noise made by the keys when they are released. This is achieved by pulsing the solenoid during key release to slow the key down. This new feature is compatible with all PDS 128+ and 228 CFX Silent Drive systems, and is added by using the Flash Memory feature that allows for convenient software upgrades. To add NRC at no charge, get the PianoDisc Update 4.2 and Silent

Drive CPU Update F from the PianoDisc web site or from an authorized PianoDisc installer.

For a limited time, PianoDisc is offering five hundred dollars in free music software with each PianoDisc system purchased. See your dealer for details.

The next generation PianoDisc system, Opus7, has just been released in 2004. In addition to the PianoDisc playback system and SymphonyPro sound module, Opus7 features a wireless, internet-ready, Web Tablet with touchscreen and full color, high resolution graphics as the system's "Conductor." It has the ability to download music and system upgrades directly from PianoDisc's website, and surf the web and receive email (broadband users only), among other features. The Opus7 system is invisible — mounted completely out of sight under the piano — but with an access panel that allows the user to connect the included floppy and CD drives for copying music to the system's "MX3" music storage hard drive beginning at 20-gigabytes in size. The MX3 hard drive comes with forty hours of pre-loaded music. Its MX3 media format will accept Standard MIDI files type 0 and 1 available from a wide variety of Standard MIDI file publishers, PianoDisc CDs, and standard audio CDs. (The company says while playback of non-PianoDisc media is supported, it is not guaranteed.) Music saved to the MX3 hard drive from diverse sources can be organized into separate "libraries" and played back from a single source for convenience. The MX3 format provides many hours of true digital stereo sound with piano accompaniment without having to change CDs.

Opus7 comes in two versions, "Opulence" and "Luxury." Opulence is the full system. Luxury is designed to integrate with home automation systems, and so does not come with the web tablet, router, or floppy and CD drives, as it is assumed that the home automation system will already include these or similar interfaces. A "Performance Package" option includes the TFT MIDI record strip, mute rail, and headphones for recording one's own playing or for use as a QuietTime system or MIDI controller. Owners of 228 CFX or PDS 128 PianoDisc systems can upgrade to Opus7 at a modest discount to the full system price. Note, however, that PianoDisc will continue to produce and sell the (current) 228 CFX system. Opus7 is distributed through an exclusive network of authorized dealers.

PianoDisc has reintroduced the AudioForte system, originally developed by Schimmel and described in an earlier editon of *The Piano Book*. AudioForte is a system of specialized speaker drivers mounted under the piano that turn a piano soundboard into spectacular stereo speakers.

PLEYEL

Pleyel pianos are now being distributed directly by the manufacturer:

Manufacture Francaise de Pianos
30319 Ales Cedex, France

(33) 4 66 56 25 00
pleyel.cial-france@wanadoo.fr
www.pleyel.fr

Pleyel has introduced a new 5' 8" model 170 grand piano. The P 118 vertical is now available in a leather finish.

PRAMBERGER

See "Young Chang"

QRS / PIANOMATION

New phone number (change of area code): 239-597-5888

QRS has made changes to its line of Pianomation player piano systems since publication of the Fourth Edition of *The Piano Book*. As mentioned in the book, Pianomation consists of a basic playback engine common to all its systems plus a choice of several different front-end controllers that determine the input to the system.

The simplest and least expensive controller is the model 2000C. The control box is hidden under the piano. It has no built-in disk drives, but instead uses your own off-the-shelf stereo components or computer to play MIDI files or QRS CDs and DVDs. The background music comes from your own stereo system, while a wireless transmitter sends the piano data to the Pianomation system, even through walls.

The model 2000CD+ is like the 2000C, above, but includes its own CD player for playing QRS audio CDs. It also comes with a speaker. Because of its "plug and play" simplicity, it is the easiest to use and most popular of the systems.

Formerly called "AMC" (Analog to MIDI Controller) and now called "Chili," this controller comes with both CD and floppy drives. The CD drive will play both audio CDs and data CDs (CD ROMs), the latter potentially containing thousands of MIDI files on a single CD. The company says this system will also play Yamaha Disklavier floppy disks, as well as Standard MIDI files type 1 and 0. It also has internal memory storage capabilities and comes with a record strip, a speaker, headphone outputs, and a sound module. Chili has both mixed and unmixed audio outputs so that the background music track and the piano track can be mixed for piping around the house, but the piano track can be omitted from the speakers located in the room containing the piano. Individual sources of audio sound can be finely adjusted so they will sound properly balanced at any volume level.

The above systems can be ordered or installed through any dealer doing business with QRS, but the company also makes two "Serenade" systems that are available only through an exclusive dealer network. Serenade CD is like the 2000CD+ system, but is only 1/2" high (for those who prefer their Pianomation to be as unobtrusive as possible) and plays both QRS audio CDs and PianoDisc CDs, according to the company. It comes with a remote control.

Serenade Pro is a fully-loaded system similar to Chili, with both floppy and CD (audio and CD ROM) drives, a sound module, record strip, and speaker, but also contains a hard drive (instead of internal memory) and a 900 mhz two-way wireless remote, has space for an optional karaoke card, and will play MP3 (live music) files. It does not have Chili's capability for both mixed and unmixed audio outputs and headphone jacks.

Sync-Along is a new feature that will play on either the Chili controller or the Serenade Pro. Similar to Yamaha's PianoSmart, QRS has prepared a piano track in MIDI format on a floppy disk to go along with each of a number of popular audio CDs and DVDs available on the general market. When the owner plays both the floppy and the CD or DVD at the same time, Sync-Along links them together, enabling Pianomation to accurately play along with the CD or DVD. A new Transcription series is similar to Sync-Along but without the background music or visual accompaniment. A solo performance audio CD or DVD is transcribed and offered as a QRS CD so the customer can hear the performance on his or her own piano.

The QRS record option used to be offered in both "LiteSwitch" and "OptiScan" versions. These have been discontinued. QRS is currently using the well-regarded Gulbransen record strip while it is developing a new generation of the OptiScan record system.

QRS has introduced its "NetPiano" service through which customers can download any of the thousands of songs from the QRS library to their Pianomation-equipped piano through their personal computer. A wireless transmitter plugged into the computer's audio jack transmits the music to the piano. The service is subscription based, costing in the vicinity of $25 per month, and allows the customer to have access to songs anytime, day or night, without having to build their own CD library. Subscriptions are available only through QRS dealers.

Apart from its player piano systems, QRS is constantly inventing new gadgets and gizmos for pianos that can be installed independently of Pianomation. Recent inventions include a Grand Mute Rail for quieting the sound of a grand piano (these have existed for verticals before, but not for grands), and a Grand Fallboard Closer that allows a grand fallboard to close gently and avoid hurting the player's fingers (available on many new pianos for some time, but not previously as an add-on accessory).

QRS has acquired the exclusive rights to manufacture and sell a Self-Tuning Piano System (which does not yet have a trade name). The company says the system will be designed into the manufacture of a piano and will allow the piano to maintain itself in tune between major tunings by a piano tuner. The system works by heating each string slightly to change its pitch. Initially the piano is tuned slightly sharp. While the system senses the pitch of each string, a tiny heating element under each string will heat it very slightly until it is lowered to the correct pitch. When the piano can no longer be tuned in this manner, it will need a regular tuning. It is expected that the system will be of particular interest to institutions. It was invented by Don A. Gilmore of Kansas City, Missouri. [This interesting-sounding system is temporarily on hold while the bugs are being worked out.]

RIDGEWOOD

Weber Piano Co., distributor of Ridgewood pianos, has gone out of business, and with it has gone the Ridgewood name. See "Weber."

RIEGER-KLOSS

The Rieger-Kloss line of pianos has been discontinued. The Bohemia Piano Co. is now making and distributing pianos under its own name. See under "Bohemia" in this section for more information.

RITMŰLLER

See under "Pearl River"

SAGENHAFT

Weber Piano Co., distributor of Sagenhaft pianos, has gone out of business, and with it has gone the Sagenhaft name. See "Weber."

SAMICK

New web site address: www.smcmusic.com

Samick Music Corporation, the North American marketing arm of the Korean company, is now known as SMC, and distributes Samick, Kohler & Campbell, Conover Cable, Hazelton Bros., Wm. Knabe (see "Knabe, Wm."), and Sohmer (see "Sohmer") pianos in North America. Under an arrangement with Baldwin, SMC temporarily distributed Chickering pianos left over from a production run never claimed and paid for by Baldwin after its bankruptcy (see "Baldwin"). Samick has also recently acquired a majority interest in the C. Bechstein company, a major German manufacturer. See under "Bechstein, C." Samick is no longer making pianos under the Bernhard Steiner name.

At press time, Samick has just acquired a 46 percent interest in its competitor Young Chang. Combined with other shareholders friendly to Samick's interests, the company has essentially gained control of Young Chang. U.S. distribution and administration of Young Chang pianos has been moved to the SMC headquarters in the Los Angeles area. Samick's primary interest in Young Chang is access to its manufacturing facility in Tianjin, China, which will allow Samick to sell pianos to the burgeoning Chinese domestic market. In addition, Samick and Young Chang will probably share manufacturing facilities in Korea, where both are operating well below capacity due to the shift in manufacturing to China and Indonesia and a declining market for pianos in Korea. Specific plans for such collaborations have not yet been announced. SMC says that the two product lines will maintain their distinct identities and dealer networks.

Samick has discontinued a number of models in its Samick, Kohler & Campbell, and Conover Cable lines and has come out with some new ones as well, both Korean and Indonesian. In general, it is continuing its trend of moving much of its production to Indonesia, while concentrating its Korean production on higher-end models. At the present time, all Samick and Conover Cable brand pianos are made in Indonesia. Regular Kohler & Campbell verticals (KC models) and grands (KCG models) are made in Indonesia, while all Kohler & Campbell Millenium series verticals (KMV) and grands (KFM) are made in Korea. All Sohmer and Knabe pianos are produced in Korea as well.

Hazelton Bros. is an occasionally-used name Samick now puts on its most inexpensive Indonesian piano line. The pianos have a laminated soundboard with a basswood core surrounded by spruce veneers, a regular (rather than slow-close) fallboard on the grands, and plainer cabinetry than the company's other lines. This piano is intended to compete with the Chinese pianos of other makers.

For its higher-end pianos, Samick is now using what it calls a "Pratt Reed Premium Action." This is not to be confused with the Pratt-Read action used in many American-made pianos in the mid to late twentieth century and eventually acquired by Baldwin. Samick says its Pratt Reed action is made in Korea and designed after the German Renner action.

SAUTER

New U.S. contact:

Chris Finger Pianos
101 2nd Avenue, P.O. Box 623
Niwot, Colorado 80544

888-244-8300
303-652-3110
www.sauter-pianos.de

SCHELL, LOTHAR (new listing)

U.S. contact:

Poppenberg & Associates
966 South Pearl Street
Denver, Colorado 80209

303-765-5775
pianopop@ix.netcom.com

Alternate contact: Shouda USA, Inc., 1224 Santa Anita Ave., Suite D, South El Monte, California 91733; phone 626-350-3800; email shoudausa@yahoo.com

Lothar Schell is a German piano designer whose techniques and designs have been used in pianos throughout the world. Lothar Schell vertical pianos used to be made by the Beijing Piano Co., but are now made in the company's new factory in Tieling, China, which began production in November 2003. The verticals are of Mr. Schell's own design. Features such as a variable thickness, solid spruce soundboard; full-length back posts; and extra points of attachment of the action to the plate are indications of attention to detail and quality in the design of the pianos. At present, Lothar Schell grands are made by the Dongbei Piano Co. and are similar to the other brands made by Dongbei. Mr. Schell says he expects one day to manufacture grands of his own design in his Tieling factory.

SCHIMMEL

New address for U.S. distributor:

Schimmel Piano Corporation
577B Hackman Road
Lititz, Pennsylvania 17543

Schimmel has developed several new upright models based on a more traditional philosphy of construction. These are the F 122 (48"), S 125 (49"), and O 132 (52"). Older models in the same or similar sizes continue to be produced, however. In the older models, the plate is the main structural support and contains a pocket for the pinblock. In the new models, traditional back posts assume a greater role for support, and the pinblock and soundboard are attached to the posts. The company says that the joining of wooden structural and acoustical parts enhances the tone. The new models also incorporate duplex scaling.

Schimmel has created a "family" of redesigned grands by marrying the front end of its 7' grand to two new grand models: a 5' 7" model 169 and a 6' 3" model 189. The company says the new models have the same treble scale and action as its 7' grand, and so have a similar sound and touch. To obtain a larger soundboard, the case sides are angled slightly, a technique now applied to all the grand models. The soundboard and ribs were also modified for tonal improvement. The 6' model 182 has been discontinued. An example of the new 5' 7" grand I played was typically bright, but had very good sustain and the feel of a larger piano.

In 2002, Schimmel acquired the PianoEurope factory in Kalisz, Poland, a piano restoration facility and manufacturer of the Meyer piano brand, one not generally found in the U.S. Schimmel is using this factory to launch its "Vogel" brand, a less expensive line named after the company's co-president. Schimmel says that although the skill level of the employees is high, lower wages and other lower costs will result in a piano approximately thirty percent less costly than the Schimmel. Vogel pianos will feature Renner actions and other parts from Schimmel or local Polish suppliers. Schimmel may gradually introduce older Schimmel scales into the Vogel pianos.

SCHUBERT

U.S. distribution of the Schubert pianos from Belarus has been discontinued. At dealer request, the Schubert name is now sometimes used on inexpensive pianos from China.

SCHULZE POLLMANN

New phone number for U.S. distributor: 845-429-0106

Schulze Pollmann has introduced a new 5' 3" model 160 grand. It comes with a Detoa action, but can be ordered with a Renner action at additional cost. The 46" model 117 vertical has a new scale design with agraffes and has been redesignated as model 118/P8. The 50" model 126E has been similarly redesigned and is now called 126P6.

SEILER

New U.S. contact information for Seiler:

888-621-1137
america@seiler-pianos.com
www.seiler-pianos.com

All Seiler grand models have been redesigned with a duplex scale, longer strings, larger soundboard area, longer keys, and a lighter touch. 5' 11" model 180 has become 6' 1" model 186; 6' 9" model 206 has become 6' 10" model 208; and 8' model 240 has become 8' model 242; and there is a new 9' 1" concert grand model 278. I have had an opportunity to play models 208 and 242 (the other models are brand new). Musically, both of these redesigned models are very successful. They retain the typical Seiler clarity, but with longer sustain and a marvelously even-feeling touch — a real pleasure to play.

Seiler has introduced its "Value Added Warranty." The warranty states that at the end of ten years from the date of purchase, a purchaser who has maintained his or her Seiler piano as required under the terms of the warranty may trade it in toward a new Seiler and receive a credit of the full original purchase price paid.

Seiler says that if there is no Seiler dealer in the customer's area, the customer can contact the U.S. representative to arrange for a direct purchase from Germany.

Correction: Seiler makes approximately 2,000 pianos a year.

SEJUNG (new listing)

America Sejung Corporation
295 Brea Canyon Road
Walnut, California 91789

909-839-0757
866-473-5864
sales@ASCpianos.com
www.ASCpianos.com

Pianos made by: Sejung Corp., Quingdao, China

Names used: Sejung, Falcone, Hobart M. Cable, Geo. Steck, Vivace

Sejung is a Korean-based textile, construction, and information technology business that was established in 1974, but the musical instrument portion of the business began only in 2001. In that year, the company's chairman received a proposal from an old friend with extensive experience in piano and guitar manufacturing to enter those businesses in a big way by manufacturing in China. Within a year, the company had partnered with a Chinese manufacturer (necessary for doing business in China); built a 700,000 square foot factory in Quingdao, a port city on the Eastern coast with a temperate climate; hired dozens of manufacturing managers who had once worked for Young Chang and Samick, and staffed the factory with some 2,000 workers, whom the company also feeds and houses in dormitories (necessary to attract good labor and reduce turnover). Although wages are incredibly low in China (less than one dollar per hour), the company says it has invested millions in automated production equipment in areas where precision counts, rather than just rely on cheap labor. The company produces just about every piano component in its own factories, and has a goal of producing 1,000 grand pianos and 2,000 verticals per month.

The first pianos from Sejung were shown in the U.S. in early 2003, less than one year after production began. I and other technicians examined a number of instruments at a trade show. Although still a little rough, they were definitely competent, and remarkably good for having been only an idea in someone's head less than two years earlier! The general consensus seems to be that Sejung will have little trouble bringing its quality up to that of the other Chinese manufacturers, and ahead of some, in a very short time, and is destined to be a major force in the world piano market.

For marketing the pianos in the U.S., Sejung has licensed the Falcone and Geo. Steck names from PianoDisc/Mason & Hamlin and the Hobart M. Cable name from Story & Clark (see "Mason & Hamlin" and "Story & Clark" in *The Piano Book*). The name Vivace was used briefly but is being discontinued. Initially, the pianos were sold primarily under the Falcone and Hobart M. Cable names, and the two lines were very similar. When use of the Geo. Steck name began in early 2004, that and the Hobart M. Cable pianos became similar (with some style differences), and the Falcone line was upgraded slightly. Specifically, most of the Falcone models have a slow-close fallboard, cast pedals and maple trapwork on the verticals, and slightly nicer cabinets. The Sejung name is used less often than the other names.

For model and price information, see under "Falcone," "Cable, Hobart M.," "Steck, Geo.," and "Sejung" in the Model and Pricing Guide section of this *Supplement*.

Warranty: The plate and pinblock are warranted to the original purchaser for as long as he or she owns the piano. The rest of the piano has a twelve year warranty on parts and ten years on labor. The warranty is not transferable.

SHERMAN CLAY

Correction: I have been told that for much of the 1970s and 1980s, pianos sold under the Sherman Clay label were made by Kimball or Aeolian. In the mid to late 1980s, some Sherman Clay pianos were made by Daewoo (Sojin).

SOHMER (& CO.)

Pianos are again being made under this venerable name, once considered among the finest of American-built instruments. However, there appears to be a dispute over the ownership of the Sohmer trademark, with pianos bearing this name being manufactured and distributed by two different companies.

SMC, distributor of Samick pianos, says it holds a license from the Burgett brothers, owners of PianoDisc, to use the Sohmer name. The Burgetts acquired the Sohmer trademark registrations when they purchased the assets of Mason & Hamlin out of bankruptcy in 1996. A distributor doing business under the name Persis International, Inc., who applied for the Sohmer trademark in 2001, claims that the registrations acquired by the Burgetts are expired, that the trademark had been legally abandoned by not being used since the 1994 closing of the Sohmer factory in Pennsylvania, and that the Burgetts' application to re-register was refused. SMC and the Burgetts argue that the Sohmer trademark has been in almost continuous use for more than 130 years, that the Burgetts never had any intention of abandoning it and have proof that they did not abandon it, and that the government erred in canceling its prior registration and in not approving its new application. Documents received from the U.S. Patent and Trademark Office confirm that the government considers all past registrations of the Sohmer trademark to be expired or canceled and that the Burgetts' new application was refused, subject to appeal. Further action on Persis' application has been temporarily suspended pending the Burgetts' appeal. At press time, the application process was still ongoing and it may be some time before the issue is settled for good. In the meantime, piano shoppers may find two "Sohmer" pianos in the marketplace. (Note: Persis' pianos are labeled "Sohmer" and SMC's are labeled "Sohmer & Co.") Both companies submitted product information, including model and price data, for this *Supplement*.

Persis International, Inc.
3540 N. Southport #116
Chicago, Illinois 60657

800-445-0695

Sohmer pianos from this distributor are manufactured by Royale, a Korean firm that is descended from the now-defunct joint venture between Ibach and Daewoo (see "Ibach"). Models include a 50" vertical and 5' 3", 5' 10", and 7' 2" grands. The distributor says the pianos have high quality components, such as Renner actions, Abel hammers, Delignit pinblocks, and Ciresa soundboards.

SMC
18521 Railroad St.
City of Industry, California 91748

800-592-9393
626-964-4700
www.smcmusic.com

Sohmer & Co. pianos from this distributor are made in Korea by Samick. The Sohmer & Co. model 34, a 42" vertical, features full-length backposts, a sand-cast plate, exposed 16-ply pinblock, and a slow-close fallboard—virtually identical (except for the slow-close fallboard) to the original, highly regarded Sohmer & Co. console. Sohmer & Co. grands are based on the pianos Samick made for Baldwin under the Chickering label. They have maple outer rims, sand-cast plates, spruce beams, solid brass hardware, agraffes, lacquer finishes, and other higher quality features, and are available in a variety of furntiure styles.

STECK, GEO.

PianoDisc has discontinued its Geo. Steck line of PianoDisc-equipped, Chinese-made pianos. The name has been licensed to new Chinese manufacturer Sejung. See "Sejung."

STEINBERG, GERH.

See "Perzina, Gebr."

STEINBERG, WILH.

New North American Agent:

Wilh. Steinberg Pianos North America
717 N. Saint Asaph Street
Alexandria, Virginia 22314

703-739-2220
800-440-4275
cathyharl@aol.com

The name of the manufacturer has changed from Wilhelm Steinberg Pianofortefabrik Gmbh to Thüringer Pianoforte GmbH. The company has also sold its key-making business to Kluge, now part of Steinway.

Steinberg says it will not be making the 49" vertical available with a Fandrich action, as mentioned in *The Piano Book*.

The warranty has been changed to five years, parts and labor.

Although not rated in *The Piano Book*, Wilh. Steinberg pianos, both grand and vertical, are well made and would probably be rated in Group 2.

Correction: *The Piano Book* says that the Wilh. Steinberg grand is identical to the Steingraeber grand. Although the Steinberg grand evolved from the Steingraeber, unlike the Steingraeber, the Steinberg has a duplex scale, as well as a different method of rim construction and a different bridge design.

"Eisenberg" is a new, lower-priced line from Steinberg, made in cooperation with other European factories. The former 48" Steinberg model C2, with a simpler cabinet and a different soundboard than the other Steinberg models, is expected to be part of the new line. At press time, prices and models were not yet firm.

STEINER, BERNHARD

Samick is no longer making pianos under this name.

STEINGRAEBER & SÖHNE

Additional web site address: www.steingraeber.de

Steingraeber has a new 8' 11" concert grand, model E-272.

Steingraeber is known for its many innovative technical improvements to the piano. One new one is a cylindrical knuckle (grand piano part) that revolves when played softly. It acts like a normal knuckle during normal and hard playing, but the revolving knuckle makes pianissimo playing easier, smoother, and more accurate. Another is a new action for upright pianos. The "DFM" action, as it is called, contains no springs, and is now available in the model 130 vertical.

Steingraeber has entered the high-end loudspeaker manufacturing business in conjunction with a Bayreuth company.

STEINLAGER (new listing)

A-440 Pianos
4100 Steve Reynolds Blvd., Suite F
Norcross, Georgia 30093

770-717-8047
888-565-5648

pianomen@earthlink.net
www.A440pianos.com

Steinlager pianos are made in China by Sejung (see "Sejung") and are similar to Sejung's Hobart M. Cable and Geo. Steck pianos.

STEINWAY & SONS

Steinway has launched its new Legendary Collection—one-of-a-kind reproductions of historical art case pianos—with a reproduction of the famous Alma Tadema art case Steinway. Commissioned in the 1880s by Henry Marquand, then-president of the Metropolitan Museum of Art in New York, this piano was designed and created by the famous English design firm of Sir Lawrence Alma-Tadema. In 1997, it was purchased at Sotheby's for $1,200,000. Offered at a price of $675,000, the reproduction, like the original, contains just about every possible art case decoration possible, including elaborate carvings, 17 different levels of decorative moldings, medallions, engravings, inlaid mother-of-pearl, marquetry, goatskin parchment, a frieze consisting of more than 6,000 parts, and even an oil painting. It is considered the most expensive piano ever built.

As mentioned in *The Piano Book*, Steinway has made small design changes to its vertical pianos to make them easier to tune, including shortening the tuning pin length, reducing string bearing angles, correcting alignment problems in the plate, and adding string-stretching operations at the factory. Some technicians report that the vertical pianos now tune with the same ease as other brands. Steinway is also now shipping all ebony, mahogany, and walnut verticals with artist benches.

This past year Steinway commemorated its 150th anniversary with numerous events, concerts, publications, and several new art case pianos. Each year brings stunning new instruments in the Art Case Collection. They can be viewed on Steinway's web site, www.steinway.com.

As mentioned in *The Piano Book*, Steinway maintains a restoration facility at its factory for the rebuilding of older Steinway pianos. Taking a cue from other firms that market "certified pre-owned" products, Steinway is now making these "Heirloom Collection Steinways" available through its dealer network. This program is designed to assist Steinway dealers in competing with rebuilders of older Steinways. The restored pianos will be identified by a medallion and will carry the same warranty as a new piano.

Correction: On page 206 of *The Piano Book*, I wrote that Steinway operated its own plate foundry until about 1930. My sources now tell me that the foundry operated until about 1939 or 1940.

STORY & CLARK

Web site address: www.storyandclark.com

In part due to economic factors and in part because of the problems of Baldwin, a principal supplier of parts, Story & Clark has ceased all its U.S. piano production. Pianos bearing the Story & Clark name are now made in China by the Dongbei piano factory, except for the upright models 120 and 140, which are made by Beijing Heintzmann. The Dongbei grands that are being outfitted with a QRS player piano system are pre-slotted and modified at the factory to accept the player system without cutting into the keys and keyframe. All pianos go the the Story & Clark facility in Pennsylvania for inspection and adjustment before being shipped to U.S. dealers.

STRAUSS

This brand improved somewhat before distribution was discontinued.

SUZUKI (new listing)

Suzuki Corporation
P.O. Box 261030
San Diego, California 92196

800-854-1594
858-566-9710
www.suzukimusic.com

Suzuki Corporation, the world's largest producer of musical instruments for education, has entered the acoustic piano business with a line of verticals and grands made in China by Dongbei. The pianos feature solid spruce soundboards, German Delignit pinblocks, and German Roslau strings.

VOGEL

See "Schimmel"

WALTER, CHARLES R.

New phone number (area code change): 574-266-0615

Web site address: www.walterpiano.com

Walter says he has made some changes to his vertical pianos to better control tuning pin torque (tightness), to reduce the incidence of false beats in the treble, and to smooth out the break between tenor and bass.

Release of a 5' 8" grand is scheduled for late 2004.

WEBER

SMC
18521 Railroad Street
City of Industry, California 91748

626-964-4700
800-592-9393

The Weber Piano Co. described in *The Piano Book* ceased operations in 2004. The company's owner, Samsung, licensed the Weber name from Young Chang and was required by the terms of their contract to purchase all pianos bearing that name from Young Chang. In addition, it only had the rights to sell Weber pianos in North and South America. Given these restrictions, Weber found it impossible to turn a profit in a changing business environment involving the existence of numerous new Chinese companies. Samsung first tried to purchase the Weber name from Young Chang, and then to distance itself from Young Chang by starting up a "Behning" line of pianos made in China by Sejung. These efforts proved unsuccessful, however, resulting in the decision to close Weber rather than continue to lose money. Samsung will continue to honor Weber warranties through Meadowlands Piano Co. (the new name for its piano division), which continues to answer the phone number for Weber listed in *The Piano Book* (201-902-0920).

Now that Samsung's license to use the Weber name has terminated, and Young Chang is controlled by Samick (see "Samick" and "Young Chang"), the Weber name is expected to resurface soon on a line of pianos made by Young Chang/Samick in their factories in Korea, Indonesia, and China. Models and prices had not yet been announced at press time.

WHELPDALE, MAXWELL & CODD

This company was renamed The British Piano Manufacturing Company Ltd. See under that name for more information. The company ceased operations in April 2003.

WOODCHESTER

Woodchester was purchased by Whelpdale, Maxwell & Codd, later called The British Piano Manufacturing Company Ltd., which ceased operations in April 2003. See under "British" for more information.

WYMAN (new listing)

Wyman Piano Company LLC
P.O. Box 218802
Nashville, Tennessee 37221

615-356-9143
info@wymanpiano.com
www.wymanpiano.com

Wyman Piano Company is a new venture created by experienced former Baldwin executives. The Wyman line consists of six vertical piano sizes (including a 39" 73-note model) and four grand sizes in a variety of cabinet styles and finishes. All are manufactured in China by the Beijing Xinghai Piano Company (see "Beijing Xinghai"). The verticals are probably similar to the ones made by Beijing under the Ellington name and sold until recently by Baldwin, but with cabinetry differences (see "Baldwin"). Wyman says that its executives make frequent trips to Beijing to monitor manufacturing and inspect finished instruments. The pianos come with a ten-year parts and labor warranty.

XINGHAI

See "Beijing Xinghai"

YAMAHA
including Disklavier

Yamaha has replaced its 4' 11" model GA1 grand and corresponding Disklavier model DGA1 with less expensive, Indonesian-made versions, models GA1E and DGA1E, respectively.

Perhaps in response to criticisms of the tone of its 5' 3" GH1B series of grands (or perhaps because the introduction of an inexpensive piano from Indonesia has made the low-priced 5' 3" pianos redundant), Yamaha has replaced the GH1B series, and the less-expensive variant model GP1, with a new 5' 3" GC1 series. The new models feature the same scale design, duplex scaling, and tone collector construction as the more expensive C1 series, but with a bass sustain pedal instead of a sostenuto, and with less expensive cabinetry and plate finish. The price of the GC1 is about the same as the GH1B and it is available in most of the same furniture styles and finishes. A Disklavier version of the GC1, the DGC1A, replaces the corresponding Disklavier versions of the GH1B and GP1 pianos being discontinued.

The model C1 "Metro" and its Disklavier counterpart are special centennial edition pianos with a unique rim design in polished ebony and champagne gold. They mark the 100th anniversary of the first Yamaha grand.

Model M475 is a new 44" console with cabinetry sophistication halfway between models M450 and M500. Fancy furniture versions of the popular P22 studio are now offered as model P600. Upright models U1 and U3 now sport a longer music desk—a very welcome addition. Model U3 joins model U5 in the use of a "floating" soundboard support system—the soundboard is not completely attached to the back at the top, allowing it to vibrate a little more freely for enhanced tonal performance.

The "A" at the end of most Disklavier model designations refers to the new CD (audio) function in these instruments, one of the Mark III (i.e., third generation) Disklavier features. Disklavier grands are no longer available without the CD function, except for model DGA1E and DGC1. Most Disklavier verticals don't have the CD function; however, it can be added. DCD1 is an add-on CD drive that can be added to any Disklavier grand or vertical, new or old.

The model DU1A is a new Disklavier version of the 48" U1 upright. It is the only Disklavier upright with Mark III features. It replaces both the MX1Z Disklavier and the MPX1Z Disklavier with Silent Feature. The DU1A contains the Silent Feature; a version of this model without the Silent Feature is no longer offered. The 48" MIDIPiano model MP1Z will become the MPU1.

Disklavier Pro models now have all the Mark III Disklavier features (except built-in speakers), including the CD drive, 16 MB of flash memory, and SmartKey and CueTime.

PianoSmart technology is a new feature of all Mark III Disklavier pianos. Yamaha has prepared a piano track in MIDI format on a floppy disk to go along with each of a number of popular audio CDs available on the general market. When the owner plays both the floppy and the CD at the same time, PianoSmart links them together, enabling the Disklavier to accurately play along with the CD. One can also record a piano accompaniment to a favorite audio CD. Pop the CD and a blank floppy into a Mark III Disklavier and record yourself playing along. The two will then be linked together for future playback. PianoSmart is available as a free software upgrade from Yamaha. The "smart" MIDI files will be added to the library of Disklavier musical offerings available from Yamaha. Customers with older Disklavier versions can retrofit PianoSmart into their system by buying the DCD1 Disklavier CD player and a software upgrade, although it may require a memory upgrade as well.

In late 2004, Yamaha is expected to release the Mark IV version of the Disklavier. It will contain: an 80 gigabyte hard drive capable of holding all the Disklavier software ever written (and then some!); a tablet or pocket remote control to communicate wirelessly with the Disklavier; built-in ethernet for connecting to your network and downloading MIDI files; the ability to play much softer as a result of a higher-speed CPU, greater MIDI resolution, and improved solenoids; more sensitive recording capabilities due to the use of greyscale (continuous) hammershank and key sensors; karaoke capability, pitch correction, an improved speaker system; and more. Playback-only models will continue to use the Mark III system. Detailed specifications, models, and prices for the Mark IV Disklavier were not yet available at press time.

To help its dealers overcome competition from "grey market" pianos, Yamaha has begun an "Heirloom Assurance" program that provides a five-year warranty on a used Yamaha piano less than twenty-five years old purchased from an authorized Yamaha dealer. Obviously, the instrument must be a Yamaha originally manufactured for the U.S. market. For the piano to be eligible for the warranty, the dealer must first submit technical information about the piano's condition to Yamaha and gain the company's approval.

YOUNG CHANG
including Bergmann and Pramberger

New U.S. distributor information:

AND Music Corporation
c/o SMC
18521 Railroad Street
City of Industry, California 91748

626-964-4700
800-592-9393

Young Chang America has changed its corporate name to AND Music Corporation.

At press time, Young Chang's competitor, Samick, has just gained a controlling interest in Young Chang and has moved Young Chang's U.S. administrative headquarters to Samick's in Los Angeles. Samick says it intends to maintain separate identites and dealer networks for the two brands.

In *The Piano Book*, I stated that Young Chang was retiring its "Gold" series in favor of its Pramberger Signature series. The Gold series has now been resurrected as Young Chang's upper-level Chinese line from its factory in Tianjin, China. Model numbers begin with "G." It differs from the company's Bergmann line (also made in China) as follows: Warranty (twelve years on Young Chang "Gold," ten years on Bergmann); cosmetic differences in legs, casters, plate color, inner rim color, lid, other cabinetry; tapered soundboard and upgraded hammers on Young Chang "Gold" grands; laminated soundboard on Bergmann verticals, solid spruce soundboard on Young Chang "Gold" verticals.

All Bergmann model numbers now begin with "B," the grands with "BTG." A new 5' 9" model BTG-175 and 6' 1" model BTG-185, both made in China, are based on the scales of the corresponding Young Chang "Gold" series pianos.

Young Chang says it has changed the front duplex scale on all its grand models to a new configuration for a cleaner sound.

Additions to the Pramberger "Platinum Edition" series now includes a 52" model JP-52 upright and a 7' 6" model JP-228 grand. Beginning in 2003, all Pramberger grands come with a Pramberger/Renner action (Renner parts on a Pramberger action frame), including the damper action. These actions can be identified by their wooden action rail and the Renner label.

The Kurzweil Player System (KPS) is similar to the QRS Chili system when installed in Young Chang pianos. When installed in Bergmann pianos, the KPS is only available as the QRS 2000 CD + system.

OTHER ITEMS OF INTEREST

MOOG PIANO BAR

Moog Music Inc.
554C Riverside Drive
Asheville, North Carolina 28801

828-251-0090

info@moogmusic.com
www.moogmusic.com

Moog Music Inc., founded by electronic music pioneer Robert Moog, has introduced an amazingly simple and elegant way of turning any acoustic piano into a MIDI controller without modifying the piano in any way. The system consists of three parts: A *scanner bar* sits on the cheek blocks, spanning the keyboard immediately in front of the fallboard and slightly above the keys. Optical sensors in the scanner bar measure the movement of the keys and translate it into note and velocity information. A *pedal sensor* rests beneath the pedals and detects their motion. A *control module* sits on the piano, receiving the data from the scanner bar and pedal sensor, turning it into MIDI information that can trigger over 300 built-in sounds. The control module can hold up to 100 setups, twenty of which can be stored on a portable "library card," twenty that are factory-supplied, and sixty that are user-determined. The control module also contains a headphone jack, audio outputs, and MIDI in and out ports. The Moog Piano Bar is completely portable and comes with a carrying case. It sells for about $1,495 from piano dealers.

PIANO LOVERS TOUR

Piano Lovers Tour Inc.
159 Parkhill Blvd.
Melbourne, Florida 32904

321-725-5690
888-725-6633
www.PianoTour.com

Classical pianist, piano importer and dealer Brian Gatchell and his wife Ginny lead tours through historic Germany "for people who love pianos, music, history, great food & wine and beautiful sights." The tours include visits to two renowned piano factories — Feurich and Steingraeber — as well as city tours, concerts, museums, wine tastings, and other attractions. Accomodations include castle hotels. The *in-depth tour* includes a long list of attractions, and accommodations at four-star hotels. The *leisure tour* goes at a slower pace, visiting a shorter list of attractions; accommodations are at two- and three-star hotels. Both tours allow time for exploring on one's own. There is also a tour for piano technicians. For tour details, see contact information above.

MODEL and PRICING GUIDE

This guide contains the "list price" for nearly every brand, model, style, and finish of new piano that has regular distribution in the United States and, for the most part, Canada. Some marginal, local, or "stencil" brands are omitted. Except where indicated, prices are in U.S. dollars and the pianos are assumed to be for sale in the U.S. (Canadians will find the information useful after translation into Canadian dollars, but there may be differences in import duties and sales practices that will affect retail prices.) Prices and specifications are, of course, subject to change. Most manufacturers revise their prices at least once a year; two or three times a year is not uncommon when currency exchange rates are unstable. The prices in this edition were compiled in the spring of 2004.

Note that prices of most European pianos vary with the value of the dollar against the Euro. For this *Supplement*, the exchange rate used was Euro = $1.20. All prices are "landed" prices, i.e., including import duties and costs of freight to the U.S. warehouse or port of entry. However, such costs will vary depending on the shipping method employed, the port of entry, and other variables.

Some terms used in this guide require special explanation and disclaimers:

List Price

The list price is usually a starting point for negotiation, not a final sales price. The term "list price," as used in this *Supplement*, is a "standard" or "normalized" list price computed from the published wholesale price according to a formula commonly used in the industry. Some manufacturers use a different formula, however, for their own suggested retail prices, usually one that raises the prices above "standard" list by ten to fifteen percent so that their dealers can advertise a larger "discount" without losing profit. For this reason, price-shopping by comparing discounts from the manufacturers' own suggested retail prices may result in a faulty price comparison. To provide a level playing field for comparing prices, all prices in this guide are computed according to a uniform "standard" formula, *even though it may differ from the manufacturers' own suggested retail prices.* Where my list prices and those of a manufacturer differ, then, no dishonesty should be inferred; we simply employ different formulas. For most brands, but not all, the price includes a bench and the standard manufacturer's warranty for that brand (see *The Piano Book* for details). Prices for some European brands do not include a bench. Most dealers will also include moving and one or two tunings in the home, but these are optional and a matter of agreement between you and the dealer.

Style and Finish

Unless otherwise indicated, the cabinet style is assumed to be "traditional" and is not stated. Exactly what "traditional" means varies from brand to brand. In general, it is a "classic" styling with minimal embellishment and straight legs. The vertical pianos have front legs, which are free-standing on smaller verticals and attached to the cabinet with toe blocks on larger verticals. "Continental" or European styling refers to vertical pianos without decorative trim and usually without front legs. Other furniture styles (Chippendale, French Provincial, Queen Anne, etc.) are as noted. The manufacturer's own trademarked style name is used when an appropriate generic name could not be determined.

Unless otherwise stated, all finishes are assumed to be "satin," which reflects light but not images. "Polished" finishes, also known as "high-gloss" or "high-polish," are mirror-like. "Oiled" finishes are usually matte (not shiny). "Open-pore" finishes, common on some European pianos, are slightly "grainier" satin finishes due to the wood pores not being filled in prior to finishing. In fact, many finishes labeled "satin" on European pianos are actually open-pore. "Ebony" is a black finish.

Special-order–only styles and finishes are in italics.

Some descriptions of style and finish may be slightly different from the manufacturer's own for the purpose of clarity, consistency, saving space, or other reason.

Size

The height of a vertical piano is measured from the floor to the top of the piano. The length of a grand piano is measured from the very front (keyboard end) to the very back (tail end).

About Actual Selling or "Street" Prices

Buying a piano is something like buying a car—the list price is deliberately set high in anticipation of negotiating.[*] But sometimes this is

---

[*] A relatively small number of dealers have non-negotiable prices.

carried to extremes, as when the salesperson reduces the price three times in the first fifteen minutes to barely half the sticker price. In situations like this, the customer, understandably confused, is bound to ask in exasperation, "What is the *real* price of this piano?"

Unfortunately, there *is* no "real" price. In theory, the dealer pays a wholesale price and then marks it up by an amount sufficient to cover the overhead and produce a profit. In practice, however, the markup can vary considerably from sale to sale depending on such factors as:

- how long the inventory has been sitting around, racking up finance charges for the dealer

- how much of a discount the dealer received at the wholesale level for buying in quantity or for paying cash

- the dealer's cash flow situation

- the competition in that particular geographic area for a particular brand or type of piano

- special piano sales events taking place in the area

- how the salesperson sizes up your situation and your willingness to pay

- the level of pre- and post-sale service the dealer seeks to provide

- the dealer's other overhead expenses

It's not unusual for one person to pay fifty percent more than another for the same brand and model of piano—sometimes even from the same dealer on the same day! It may seem as if pricing is so chaotic that no advice can be given, but in truth, enough piano sales do fall within a certain range of typical profit margins that some guidance is possible as long as the reader understands the limitations inherent in this kind of advice.

Historically, discounts from "standard" list price have averaged ten or fifteen percent in the piano business. In recent years, however, conditions have changed such that, according to some industry sources, the average discount from list has increased to twenty or twenty-five percent. Essentially, due to growing competition from used pianos and digital pianos, and a decrease in the cultural importance attached to having a piano in the home, there are too many dealers of new pianos chasing after too few consumer dollars. In addition, higher labor costs in some parts of the world and unfavorable international currency values make some brands so expensive in the U.S. that they can only be sold at very large discounts. I think, too, that consumers are becoming more savvy and are shopping around. Unfortunately, the overhead costs of running a traditional piano store are so high that most dealers cannot stay in business if they sell at an average discount from "standard" list price of more than about twenty percent. To survive, dealers are evolving multiple new approaches: becoming more efficient, instituting low-price/high volume strategies, cutting their overhead—sometimes including service—or subsidizing their meager sales of new pianos with used pianos (which command higher profit margins), rentals, rebuilding, and other products and services.

Although the average discount has increased, it is by no means uniform. Some brands dependably bring top dollar; others languish or the price is highly situational. I did consider giving a typical range of "street" prices for each brand and model listed in this volume, but concluded that the task would be too daunting due to the extreme variation that can exist from one situation to another, and because of the political fallout that would likely result from dealers and manufacturers who fear the loss of what little power they still have over aggressive, price-shopping customers. So, for now, I've decided just to give general advice in print. (For those who desire more specific information on "street" prices, I offer additional services, such as private telephone consultations and a Pricing Guide Service on the internet. See my web site, **www.pianobook.com**, for more information.)

One way some manufacturers assist dealers in overcoming downward price pressure is to publish wholesale price lists that are less than honest. That is, dealers are routinely offered large discounts (ten percent or more) from the published wholesale price if they buy in sufficient quantity, or for certain models, or for any other reason the manufacturer can think of. Since the prices in this *Supplement* are calculated from the published wholesale prices, this practice results in over-inflated list prices in this book for those particular companies, allowing dealers of those brands to advertise larger "discounts" without losing profit. This practice is especially common among some Chinese and Korean companies, but seems to be spreading. (Most manufacturers offer small discounts from the published wholesale price list from time to time or for paying cash, but lately some manufacturers seem to be carrying this practice to greater heights.) The problem for the consumer is that these wholesale discounts are not given out uniformly by manufacturers or among dealers, another reason why an appropriate "street" price figured from the price information presented here will have to remain a rough estimate.

It should be clearly understood that the advice given here is based on my own observations, subjective judgment, and general understanding of the piano market, *not* on statistical sales data or scientific analysis. (Brand-by-brand statistical sales data are virtually nonexistent.) This knowledge is the product of discussions with hundreds of customers, dealers, technicians, and industry executives over the years. Other industry observers may come to different conclusions. This rundown of "street" prices won't cover every brand, but should give a rough idea of what to expect and the ability to predict prices for some of the brands not specifically covered. I can't emphasize enough, however, that pricing can be highly situational, dependent on the mix of available products and the ease of comparison shopping in any particular geographic area, as well as on the financial situation of dealer and customer. The following generalizations should prove useful to you, but expect almost anything.

As a general rule of thumb:

• the more expensive the piano, the higher the possible discount

• the more "exclusive" a brand is perceived to be, the less likely head-to-head competition, and therefore the lower the possible discount

• the longer a piano remains unsold, the higher the possible discount

• the more service-intensive the piano, the lower the possible discount

Although discounts from "standard" list price for most Japanese and Korean pianos typically start at perhaps fifteen percent, twenty or even thirty percent discounts are not uncommon in a moderately competitive environment, especially if the dealer knows the customer is shopping around. Chinese and Indonesian pianos, on the other hand, are so inexpensive, and some still require so much servicing by the dealer, that it's simply not cost-effective to sell them for much less than full list price. Expect little or no discount. Some dealers just use them as "loss leaders," that is, just to get people into the store, whereupon the customer is sold on a more expensive piano.

The Boston piano, although manufactured in Japan, is generally viewed as being a little more "exclusive" due to its association with Steinway, so deep discounting is much less likely. Discounts in the range of ten percent or so are common. Baldwin, whose pianos are usually seen as being distinctly different from the Asian products even though they often share common price ranges, also benefits from exceptional name recognition and its historical "made in USA" connection. Discounting is likely to be moderate, in my experience—perhaps fifteen to twenty-five percent. (Note: Due to Baldwin's recent bankruptcy and sale, however, discounting has tended to be larger than usual during the past couple of years. Until this situation settles down, some very large discounts may be possible on Baldwin products in selected situations.)

Western European instruments tend to be extremely expensive here due to their high quality, the high European cost of doing business, additional middlemen/importers and, recently, unfavorable exchange rates. There appear to be two types of dealers of these pianos. One type, specializing in selling higher-quality instruments to a demanding clientele, manages to get top dollar for them despite their high price, with discounts averaging only twenty percent or so. They are not particularly into negotiating. The other type of dealer, probably more numerous, depends for his or her "bread and butter" on consumer-grade pianos and is pleased to make a relatively small profit on the occasional sale of a luxury instrument. Discounts here may well approach thirty to forty percent at times, especially if the piano has gone unsold for an extended period of time. Eastern European brands like Petrof and Estonia are already seen as being a good deal for the money, so expect moderate discounts—perhaps fifteen to twenty-five percent.

Steinway pianos have always been in a class by themselves, historically the only expensive piano to continually command high profit margins. Except for older Steinways and the occasional Mason & Hamlin, Steinway has little competition and fewer than one hundred dealers in the United States. Service requirements can be quite high, at least in part because of the higher standards often required to satisfy a fussier clientele. Historically, Steinway pianos have sold at or near full list price. (Some dealers even sell *above* list!) This is still true in many places, but in recent years I have seen a little more discounting than in the past. Ten to fifteen percent is not unusual in some areas; as much as twenty percent would be rare.

For brands not mentioned or implied in the above discussion, it's usually a safe bet to figure a discount of fifteen to twenty-five percent from the prices in this *Supplement*, with greater discounts possible in selected situations.

There is no "fair" price for a piano except the one the buyer and seller agree on. The dealer is no more obligated to sell you a piano at a deep discount than you are obligated to pay the list price. Many dealers are simply not able to sell at the low end of the range consistently and still stay in business. It's understandable that you would like to pay the lowest price possible, and there's no harm in asking, but remember that piano shopping is not just about chasing the lowest price. Be sure you are getting the instrument that best suits your needs and preferences and that the dealer is committed to providing the proper pre- and post-sale service.

(Note: Remember that the "street" price discounts suggested above should be subtracted from the "standard" list prices in this *Supplement*, not from the manufacturer's suggested retail price.)

For more information on shopping for a new piano and on how to save money, please see pages 60–75 in *The Piano Book* (fourth edition).

Model	Size	Style and Finish	Price*

Albrecht, Charles

Verticals

Model	Size	Style and Finish	Price*
4300	43"	Contemporary Polished Ebony	5,100.
4300	43"	Contemporary Polished Mahogany	5,200.
4300	43"	Contemporary Walnut	4,950.
4300	43"	Contemporary Polished Walnut	5,200.
4300	43"	Contemporary Cherry	4,950.
4300	43"	Contemporary Polished Ivory	5,200.
4300	43"	Contemporary Polished White	5,200.
4403	43-1/2"	Designer Cherry	5,850.
4403	43-1/2"	Designer Brown Oak	5,850.
4406	43-1/2"	Designer Brown Oak	5,700.
4413	43-1/2"	Designer Deluxe Cherry	7,450.
4413	43-1/2"	Designer Walnut	7,250.
4507	45-1/2"	Institutional Cherry	5,200.
4507	45-1/2"	Institutional Walnut	5,200.
4513	45-1/2"	Chippendale Polished Ebony	8,100.
4513	45-1/2"	Chippendale Polished Mahogany	8,650.
4513	45-1/2"	Chippendale Polished Walnut	8,650.
4517	45-1/2"	Institutional Polished Ebony	7,000.
4517	45-1/2"	Institutional Polished Mahogany	7,550.
4517	45-1/2"	Institutional Polished Walnut	7,550.
4517	45-1/2"	Institutional Polished Ivory	5,400.
4517	45-1/2"	Institutional Polished White	5,400.
4701	47"	Designer Cherry	6,400.
4701	47"	Designer Mahogany	6,400.
4703	47"	Designer Cherry	6,400.
4703	47"	Designer Mahogany	6,400.
4706	47"	Designer Brown Oak	6,050.
4803	48"	Institutional Polished Ebony	6,500.
4803	48"	Institutional Polished Mahogany	6,900.
4907	49"	Institutional Polished Ebony	6,800.
4907	49"	Institutional Polished Mahogany	7,250.
4907	49"	Institutional Polished Walnut	7,250.
5207	51-1/2"	Institutional Ebony and Polished Ebony	8,200.
5207	51-1/2"	Institutional Polished Mahogany	8,650.
5207	51-1/2"	Institutional Polished Walnut	8,650.
5207	51-1/2"	Institutional Polished Ivory	8,200.

*For explanation of terms and prices, please see pages 54–60.

Model	Size	Style and Finish	Price*

Albrecht, Charles (continued)

Grands

Model	Size	Style and Finish	Price*
G4801	4' 8"	"Petite" Polished Ebony	13,600.
G4801	4' 8"	"Petite" Polished Mahogany	14,800.
G4801	4' 8"	"Petite" Polished Walnut	14,800.
G4801	4' 8"	"Petite" Polished White	14,050.
G5309	5' 3-1/2"	Ebony	15,900.
G5309	5' 3-1/2"	Polished Ebony	15,650.
G5309	5' 3-1/2"	Polished Mahogany	16,200.
G5309	5' 3-1/2"	Polished Walnut	16,200.
G5313	5' 3-1/2"	French Mahogany	18,900.
G5313	5' 3-1/2"	French Walnut	18,900.
G5314	5' 3-1/2"	Victorian Mahogany	17,500.
G5314	5' 3-1/2"	Victorian Walnut	17,500.
G5701	5' 7"	Ebony	18,000.
G5701	5' 7"	Polished Ebony	17,700.
G5701	5' 7"	Mahogany	18,600.
G5701	5' 7"	Polished Mahogany	18,350.
G5701	5' 7"	Polished Walnut	18,350.
G5701	5' 7"	Cherry	18,600.
G5701	5' 7"	Polished White	17,700.
G6101	6' 1"	Ebony and Polished Ebony	18,800.
G6101	6' 1"	Polished Mahogany	19,450.
G6101	6' 1"	Polished Walnut	19,450.
G7101	7'	Polished Ebony	21,800.

Astin-Weight

Verticals

Model	Size	Style and Finish	Price*
375	41"	Santa Fe Oiled Oak	8,740.
375	41"	Spanish Oiled Oak	7,980.
375	41"	Spanish Lacquer Oak	8,180.
375	41"	Italian Oiled Walnut	8,380.
375	41"	Italian Lacquer Walnut	8,580.
375	41"	Regency Oiled Oak	8,380.
375	41"	Regency Lacquer Oak	8,500.
375	41"	Regency Oiled Walnut	8,500.
375	41"	Regency Lacquer Walnut	8,520.
U-500	50"	Oiled Oak	13,380.
U-500	50"	Santa Fe Oiled Oak	14,780.

Model	Size	Style and Finish	Price*
U-500	50"	Lacquer Oak	13,780.
U-500	50"	Oiled Walnut	13,980.
U-500	50"	Lacquer Walnut	14,380.
Grands			
———	5' 9"	Ebony	35,700.

August Förster — see "Förster, August"

Baldwin

Verticals

Model	Size	Style and Finish	Price*
660E	43-1/2"	Georgian Mahogany	5,606.
662E	43-1/2"	Queen Anne Regency Cherry	5,606.
665E	43-1/2"	Transitional Country Oak	5,606.
667E	43-1/2"	Country French Oak	5,606.
2090E	43-1/2"	Hepplewhite Vintage Mahogany	6,526.
2095E	43-1/2"	Regal Oak	6,526.
2096E	43-1/2"	Queen Anne Royal Cherry	6,526.
243E	45"	Ebony	6,862.
243E	45"	Golden Oak	6,862.
243E	45"	American Walnut	6,862.
243E	45"	Lyptus Wood Clear Finish	6,862.
243Elvis	45"	Elvis Presley Signature	15,632.
GSV10	45"	Gibson Les Paul	22,568.
5050E	45"	Mahogany	9,668.
5052E	45"	Limited Edition Queen Anne Cherry	8,770.
5057E	45"	Limited Edition Georgian Oak	8,970.
5062E	45"	Queen Anne Distressed Cherry	9,668.
248E	48"	American Walnut	9,754.
6000E	52"	Ebony	12,558.
6000E	52"	Mahogany	12,850.
6000E	52"	Regency Cherry with Gold Trim	13,952.

Grands

Model	Size	Style and Finish	Price*
M1	5' 2"	Ebony	30,122.
M1	5' 2"	Polished Ebony	31,312.
M1	5' 2"	Mahogany	31,200.
M1	5' 2"	Polished Mahogany	33,532.
M1	5' 2"	Walnut	32,030.

*For explanation of terms and prices, please see pages 54–60.

Model	Size	Style and Finish	Price*

Baldwin (continued)

Model	Size	Style and Finish	Price*
M1	5' 2"	Polished Walnut	33,936.
M1	5' 2"	Polished Cherry	33,172.
225E	5' 2"	French Provincial Cherry	37,860.
R1	5' 8"	Ebony	33,890.
R1	5' 8"	Polished Ebony	35,282.
R1	5' 8"	Mahogany	35,348.
R1	5' 8"	Polished Mahogany	37,682.
R1	5' 8"	Walnut	36,314.
R1	5' 8"	Polished Walnut	38,488.
R1	5' 8"	Polished Cherry	37,592.
R1	5' 8"	Polished Bubinga	43,738.
R1	5' 8"	Polished Indian Rosewood	47,102.
R1	5' 8"	Polished Pommele	47,102.
226E	5' 8"	French Provincial Cherry	41,764.
226E	5' 8"	French Provincial Polished Cherry	43,198.
227E	5' 8"	Louis XVI Mahogany	41,764.
L1	6' 3"	Ebony	38,264.
L1	6' 3"	Polished Ebony	39,700.
L1	6' 3"	Mahogany	39,834.
L1	6' 3"	Polished Mahogany	42,234.
L1	6' 3"	Walnut	41,046.
L1	6' 3"	Polished Walnut	43,512.
L1	6' 3"	Polished Cherry	42,392.
SF10E	7'	Ebony	53,808.
SF10E	7'	Polished Ebony	55,558.
SF10E	7'	Mahogany	55,558.
SD10	9'	Ebony	86,038.
SD10	9'	Polished Ebony	92,072.

ConcertMaster (approximate, including installation by factory or dealer)

Verticals	Playback only / with Perf. Option	9,560./10,920.
Grands	Playback only / with Perf. Option	10,320./11,770.
	With stop rail, add $450	

Note: Discounts may apply, especially as an incentive to purchase the piano.

Baldwin, D.H.

Verticals

Model	Size	Style and Finish	Price*
561	43-1/2"	Lyptus Wood Clear Finish	3,790.
562	43-1/2"	Red Cherry	3,590.
562B	43-1/2"	Brown Cherry	3,590.
562D	43-1/2"	Distressed Red Cherry	3,790.
562BD	43-1/2"	Distressed Brown Cherry	3,790.
569	43-1/2"	Lyptus Wood Ebony	3,590.
570	43-1/2"	Lyptus Wood Mahogany	4,590.
572	43-1/2"	Red Cherry	4,590.
4560	45"	Lyptus Wood Mahogany	6,400.
4561	45"	Lyptus Wood Clear Finish	6,400.
4562	45"	Lyptus Wood Cherry	6,400.
4569	45"	Lyptus Wood Ebony	6,400.

Grands

Model	Size	Style and Finish	Price*
M5	5' 2"	Ebony	16,000.
M5	5' 2"	French Provincial Cherry	17,600.

Bechstein, (C.)

Models beginning with "A" say only "Bechstein" on the fallboard. Others say "C. Bechstein." See article in Manufacturer and Product Update section of this Supplement for details.

Verticals

Model	Size	Style and Finish	Price*
A-3	45-1/2"	Polished Ebony	15,780.
A-3	45-1/2"	Mahogany	15,160.
A-3	45-1/2"	Polished Mahogany	16,800.
A-3	45-1/2"	Walnut	15,160.
A-3	45-1/2"	Polished Walnut	16,800.
A-3	45-1/2"	Cherry	15,160.
A-3	45-1/2"	Polished Cherry	16,800.
A-3	45-1/2"	Alder	15,160.
A-3	45-1/2"	Beech	15,160.
A-3	45-1/2"	Polished White	16,600.
Balance	45-1/2"	Polished Ebony	27,800.
Avance	46-1/2"	Polished Ebony	34,400.
A-2	47"	Polished Ebony	17,200.
A-2	47"	Mahogany	17,000.
A-2	47"	Polished Mahogany	18,200.

*For explanation of terms and prices, please see pages 54–60.

Model	Size	Style and Finish	Price*

Bechstein, (C.) (continued)

Model	Size	Style and Finish	Price*
A-2	47"	Walnut	17,000.
A-2	47"	Polished Walnut	18,200.
A-2	47"	Cherry	17,000.
A-2	47"	Polished Cherry	18,200.
A-2	47"	Alder	16,600.
A-2	47"	Polished White	18,000.
A-1	49"	Polished Ebony	18,400.
A-1	49"	Mahogany	18,200.
A-1	49"	Polished Mahogany	19,800.
A-1	49"	Walnut	18,200.
A-1	49"	Polished Walnut	19,800.
A-1	49"	Cherry	18,200.
A-1	49"	Polished Cherry	19,800.
A-1	49"	Beech	17,200.
A-1	49"	Polished White	19,800.
Ars Nova	49"	Polished Ebony	38,700.
Concert 8	51-1/2"	Polished Ebony	48,000.
Concert 8	51-1/2"	Mahogany	48,000.
Concert 8	51-1/2"	Polished Mahogany	50,100.
Concert 8	51-1/2"	Walnut	48,000.
Concert 8	51-1/2"	Polished Walnut	50,100.
Concert 8	51-1/2"	Cherry	48,000.

Grands

Model	Size	Style and Finish	Price*
A-160	5' 3"	Ebony	44,800.
A-160	5' 3"	Polished Ebony	48,600.
A-160	5' 3"	Polished Mahogany	50,400.
A-160	5' 3"	Polished White	52,400.
A-190	6' 3"	Ebony	48,200.
A-190	6' 3"	Polished Ebony	51,900.
A-190	6' 3"	Polished Mahogany	53,700.
A-190	6' 3"	Polished White	55,800.
M/P 192	6' 4"	Ebony and Polished Ebony	98,600.
M/P 192	6' 4"	Polished Mahogany	102,800.
A-208	6' 10"	Polished Ebony	57,400.
A-208	6' 10"	Polished Mahogany	59,400.
B-210	6' 11"	Ebony and Polished Ebony	116,000.
C-232	7' 6"	Polished Ebony	140,000.
D-280	9' 2"	Polished Ebony	185,500.

Bergmann

Verticals

Model	Size	Style and Finish	Price
BE-109	43"	Continental Polished Ebony	2,840.
BE-109	43"	Continental Polished Red Mahogany	2,930.
BE-109	43"	Continental Polished Brown Mahogany	2,930.
BE-109	43"	Continental Polished Ivory	2,840.
BAF-108	43"	Mahogany	3,350.
BAF-108	43"	Queen Anne Oak	3,350.
BAF-108	43"	Mediterranean Oak	3,350.
BAF-108	43"	Queen Anne Cherry	3,350.
BAF-108	43"	French Provincial Cherry	3,350.
BE-118	47"	Polished Ebony	3,350.
BE-118	47"	Polished Red Mahogany	3,470.
BAF-118	47"	Cherry	3,840.
BE-121	48"	Polished Ebony	3,560.
BE-121	48"	Polished Red Mahogany	3,680.
BE-131	52"	Polished Ebony	3,770.
BE-131	52"	Polished Red Mahogany	3,890.

Grands

Model	Size	Style and Finish	Price
BTG-150	4' 11"	Polished Ebony	8,810.
BTG-150	4' 11"	Polished Red Mahogany	8,810.
BTG-150	4' 11"	Polished Ivory	8,810.
BTG-157	5' 2"	Polished Ebony	9,860.
BTG-157	5' 2"	Polished Red Mahogany	9,860.
BTG-157	5' 2"	Polished Ivory	9,860.
BTG-175	5' 9"	Polished Ebony	11,120.
BTG-185	6' 1"	Polished Ebony	11,960.

Blüthner

Prices do not include bench.

Verticals

Model	Size	Style and Finish	Price
I	45"	Ebony or Polished Ebony	22,531.
I	45"	Walnut or Polished Walnut	23,543.
I	45"	Mahogany or Polished Mahogany	23,420.
I	45"	Cherry or Polished Cherry	23,420.
I	45"	White or Polished White	23,543.
C	46"	Ebony or Polished Ebony	23,786.
C	46"	Walnut or Polished Walnut	25,011.

*For explanation of terms and prices, please see pages 54–60.

Model	Size	Style and Finish	Price*

Blüthner (continued)

Model	Size	Style and Finish	Price*
C	46"	Mahogany or Polished Mahogany	24,772.
C	46"	Cherry or Polished Cherry	24,891.
C	46"	White or Polished White	25,011.
C	46"	Polished Bubinga, Yew, Macassar Ebony	26,202.
C	46"	Saxony Polished Pyramid Mahogany	31,426.
C	46"	Saxony Polished Burl Walnut Inlay	31,728.
A	49"	Ebony or Polished Ebony	30,338.
A	49"	Walnut or Polished Walnut	31,853.
A	49"	Mahogany or Polished Mahogany	31,549.
A	49"	Cherry or Polished Cherry	31,703.
A	49"	White or Polished White	31,853.
A	49"	Polished Bubinga, Yew, Macassar Ebony	33,372.
A	49"	Saxony Polished Pyramid Mahogany	40,026.
A	49"	Saxony Polished Burl Walnut Inlay	40,412.
B	52"	Ebony or Polished Ebony	34,638.
B	52"	Walnut or Polished Walnut	36,369.
B	52"	Mahogany or Polished Mahogany	36,023.
B	52"	Cherry or Polished Cherry	36,194.
B	52"	White or Polished White	36,369.
B	52"	Polished Bubinga, Yew, Macassar Ebony	38,100.
B	52"	Saxony Polished Pyramid Mahogany	45,700.
B	52"	Saxony Polished Burl Walnut Inlay	46,140.
—	—	*Sostenuto pedal on vertical piano, add'l*	2,160.

Grands

Model	Size	Style and Finish	Price*
11	5' 1"	Ebony or Polished Ebony	61,424.
11	5' 1"	Walnut or Polished Walnut	64,496.
11	5' 1"	Mahogany or Polished Mahogany	63,881.
11	5' 1"	Cherry or Polished Cherry	64,189.
11	5' 1"	White or Polished White	64,496.
11	5' 1"	Polished Bubinga, Yew, Macassar Ebony	67,569.
11	5' 1"	Saxony Polished Pyramid Mahogany	81,045.
11	5' 1"	Saxony Polished Burl Walnut Inlay	81,823.
11	5' 1"	"President" Polished Ebony	68,577.
11	5' 1"	"President" Polished Mahogany	71,320.
11	5' 1"	"President" Polished Walnut	72,004.
11	5' 1"	"President" Polished Bubinga	75,434.
11	5' 1"	Louis XV Ebony or Polished Ebony	71,692.
11	5' 1"	Louis XV Mahogany or Polished Mahogany	75,278.
11	5' 1"	Louis XV Walnut or Polished Walnut	74,559.

Model	Size	Style and Finish	Price*
11	5' 1"	"Kaiser Wilhelm II" Polished Ebony	72,316.
11	5' 1"	"Kaiser Wilhelm II" Polished Mahogany	75,209.
11	5' 1"	"Kaiser Wilhelm II" Polished Walnut	75,931.
11	5' 1"	"Kaiser Wilhelm II" Polished Cherry	75,570.
11	5' 1"	"Ambassador" East Indian Rosewood	84,160.
11	5' 1"	"Ambassador" Walnut	77,927.
11	5' 1"	"Nicolas II" Walnut with Burl Inlay	84,160.
11	5' 1"	Louis XVI Rococo White with Gold	90,396.
11	5' 1"	"Classic Alexandra" Polished Ebony	69,824.
11	5' 1"	"Classic Alexandra" Polished Mahogany	73,313.
11	5' 1"	"Classic Alexandra" Polished Walnut	72,615.
10	5' 5"	Ebony or Polished Ebony	70,808.
10	5' 5"	Walnut or Polished Walnut	74,349.
10	5' 5"	Mahogany or Polished Mahogany	73,641.
10	5' 5"	Cherry or Polished Cherry	73,997.
10	5' 5"	White or Polished White	74,349.
10	5' 5"	Polished Bubinga, Yew, Macassar Ebony	77,890.
10	5' 5"	Saxony Polished Pyramid Mahogany	93,427.
10	5' 5"	Saxony Polished Burl Walnut Inlay	94,323.
10	5' 5"	"President" Polished Ebony	79,052.
10	5' 5"	"President" Polished Mahogany	82,215.
10	5' 5"	"President" Polished Walnut	83,004.
10	5' 5"	"President" Polished Bubinga	86,958.
10	5' 5"	"Senator" French Walnut with Leather	86,240.
10	5' 5"	"Senator" Jacaranda Rosewd w/Leather	91,989.
10	5' 5"	Louis XV Ebony or Polished Ebony	82,646.
10	5' 5"	Louis XV Mahogany or Pol. Mahogany	86,778.
10	5' 5"	Louis XV Walnut or Polished Walnut	85,951.
10	5' 5"	"Kaiser Wilhelm II" Polished Ebony	83,365.
10	5' 5"	"Kaiser Wilhelm II" Polished Mahogany	86,698.
10	5' 5"	"Kaiser Wilhelm II" Polished Walnut	87,531.
10	5' 5"	"Kaiser Wilhelm II" Polished Cherry	87,114.
10	5' 5"	"Ambassador" East Indian Rosewood	97,017.
10	5' 5"	"Ambassador" Walnut	89,833.
10	5' 5"	"Nicolas II" Walnut with Burl Inlay	97,017.
10	5' 5"	Louis XVI Rococo White with Gold	104,204.
10	5' 5"	"Classic Alexandra" Polished Ebony	80,490.
10	5' 5"	"Classic Alexandra" Polished Mahogany	84,514.
10	5' 5"	"Classic Alexandra" Polished Walnut	83,708.

*For explanation of terms and prices, please see pages 54–60.

Model	Size	Style and Finish	Price*

Blüthner (continued)

Model	Size	Style and Finish	Price*
6	6' 3"	Ebony or Polished Ebony	77,230.
6	6' 3"	Walnut or Polished Walnut	81,092.
6	6' 3"	Mahogany or Polished Mahogany	80,319.
6	6' 3"	Cherry or Polished Cherry	80,705.
6	6' 3"	White or Polished White	81,092.
6	6' 3"	Polished Bubinga, Yew, Macassar Ebony	84,954.
6	6' 3"	Saxony Polished Pyramid Mahogany	101,899.
6	6' 3"	Saxony Polished Burl Walnut Inlay	102,878.
6	6' 3"	"President" Polished Ebony	86,222.
6	6' 3"	"President" Polished Mahogany	89,670.
6	6' 3"	"President" Polished Walnut	90,531.
6	6' 3"	"President" Polished Bubinga	94,843.
6	6' 3"	"Senator" French Walnut with Leather	94,059.
6	6' 3"	"Senator" Jacaranda Rosewd w/Leather	100,329.
6	6' 3"	Louis XV Ebony or Polished Ebony	90,139.
6	6' 3"	Louis XV Mahogany or Polished Mahogany	94,645.
6	6' 3"	Louis XV Walnut or Polished Walnut	93,746.
6	6' 3"	"Kaiser Wilhelm II" Polished Ebony	90,923.
6	6' 3"	"Kaiser Wilhelm II" Polished Mahogany	94,559.
6	6' 3"	"Kaiser Wilhelm II" Polished Walnut	95,468.
6	6' 3"	"Kaiser Wilhelm II" Polished Cherry	95,013.
6	6' 3"	"Ambassador" East Indian Rosewood	105,815.
6	6' 3"	"Ambassador" Walnut	97,979.
6	6' 3"	"Nicolas II" Walnut with Burl Inlay	105,815.
6	6' 3"	Louis XVI Rococo White with Gold	113,655.
6	6' 3"	"Classic Alexandra" Polished Ebony	87,788.
6	6' 3"	"Classic Alexandra" Polished Mahogany	92,177.
6	6' 3"	"Classic Alexandra" Polished Walnut	91,298.
6	6' 3"	*Jubilee Edition Plate, add'l*	5,980.
4	6' 10"	Ebony or Polished Ebony	91,598.
4	6' 10"	Walnut or Polished Walnut	96,179.
4	6' 10"	Mahogany or Polished Mahogany	95,262.
4	6' 10"	Cherry or Polished Cherry	95,720.
4	6' 10"	White or Polished White	96,179.
4	6' 10"	Polished Bubinga, Yew, Macassar Ebony	100,759.
4	6' 10"	Saxony Polished Pyramid Mahogany	120,856.
4	6' 10"	Saxony Polished Burl Walnut Inlay	122,016.
4	6' 10"	"President" Polished Ebony	102,263.
4	6' 10"	"President" Polished Mahogany	106,353.

Model	Size	Style and Finish	Price*
4	6' 10"	"President" Polished Walnut	107,374.
4	6' 10"	"President" Polished Bubinga	112,488.
4	6' 10"	"Kaiser Wilhelm II" Polished Ebony	107,839.
4	6' 10"	"Kaiser Wilhelm II" Polished Mahogany	112,152.
4	6' 10"	"Kaiser Wilhelm II" Polished Walnut	113,231.
4	6' 10"	"Kaiser Wilhelm II" Polished Cherry	112,693.
4	6' 10"	"Ambassador" East Indian Rosewood	125,502.
4	6' 10"	"Ambassador" Walnut	116,207.
4	6' 10"	"Classic Alexandra" Polished Ebony	104,121.
4	6' 10"	"Classic Alexandra" Polished Mahogany	109,325.
4	6' 10"	"Classic Alexandra" Polished Walnut	108,287.
2	7' 8"	Ebony or Polished Ebony	102,374.
2	7' 8"	Walnut or Polished Walnut	107,492.
2	7' 8"	Mahogany or Polished Mahogany	106,469.
2	7' 8"	Cherry or Polished Cherry	106,982.
2	7' 8"	White or Polished White	107,492.
2	7' 8"	Polished Bubinga, Yew, Macassar Ebony	112,613.
2	7' 8"	Saxony Polished Pyramid Mahogany	135,074.
2	7' 8"	Saxony Polished Burl Walnut Inlay	136,373.
2	7' 8"	"President" Polished Ebony	114,294.
2	7' 8"	"President" Polished Mahogany	118,863.
2	7' 8"	"President" Polished Walnut	120,006.
2	7' 8"	"President" Polished Bubinga	125,721.
2	7' 8"	"Kaiser Wilhelm II" Polished Ebony	120,526.
2	7' 8"	"Kaiser Wilhelm II" Polished Mahogany	125,349.
2	7' 8"	"Kaiser Wilhelm II" Polished Walnut	126,554.
2	7' 8"	"Kaiser Wilhelm II" Polished Cherry	125,950.
2	7' 8"	"Ambassador" East Indian Rosewood	140,269.
2	7' 8"	"Ambassador" Walnut	129,877.
1	9' 2"	Ebony or Polished Ebony	122,130.
1	9' 2"	Walnut or Polished Walnut	128,237.
1	9' 2"	Mahogany or Polished Mahogany	127,016.
1	9' 2"	Cherry or Polished Cherry	127,628.
1	9' 2"	White or Polished White	128,237.
1	9' 2"	"President" Polished Ebony	136,349.
1	9' 2"	"President" Polished Mahogany	141,803.
1	9' 2"	"President" Polished Walnut	143,168.
1	9' 2"	"President" Polished Bubinga	149,983.

*For explanation of terms and prices, please see pages 54–60.

Model	Size	Style and Finish	Price*

Bohemia

Verticals

Model	Size	Style and Finish	Price*
113	45"	Polished Ebony	5,500.
113	45"	Open-pore Mahogany	5,280.
113	45"	Polished Mahogany	5,680.
113	45"	Open-pore Walnut	5,280.
113	45"	Polished Walnut	5,680.
113	45"	Open-pore Oak	5,280.
113	45"	Polished White	5,720.
118A	47"	Continental Polished Ebony	5,820.
118A	47"	Continental Open-pore Walnut	5,580.
118A	47"	Continental Polished Walnut	5,980.
118A	47"	Continental Open-pore Mahogany	5,580.
118A	47"	Continental Polished Mahogany	5,980.
118A	47"	Continental Open-pore Oak	5,580.
118A	47"	Continental Open-pore Cherry	5,820.
118A	47"	Continental Polished White	6,040.
122A	48"	Demi-Chippendale Polished Ebony	6,160.
122A	48"	Demi-Chippendale Polished Walnut	6,340.
122A	48"	Demi-Chippendale Polished Mahogany	6,340.
122A	48"	*Demi-Chippendale Pomele*	6,640.
122A	48"	Chippendale Polished Ebony	6,780.
122A	48"	Chippendale Polished Walnut	6,980.
122A	48"	Chippendale Polished Mahogany	6,980.
122A	48"	*"Romance" with Mahogany Oval*	7,140.
123A	48"	Polished Ebony	6,100.
123A	48"	Open-pore Walnut	5,840.
123A	48"	Polished Walnut	6,260.
123A	48"	Open-pore Mahogany	5,840.
123A	48"	Polished Mahogany	6,260.
123A	48"	Open-pore Oak	5,840.
123A	48"	Open-pore Cherry	6,100.
123A	48"	Polished White	6,380.
123A	48"	*Pomele*	6,460.
123A	48"	*"Exclusive" with Mahogany Oval*	6,460.
125A	49"	Polished Ebony	6,640.
125A	49"	Polished Walnut	6,840.
125A	49"	Polished Mahogany	6,840.
125A	49"	Open-pore Cherry	6,640.
125A	49"	Polished White	6,920.

Model	Size	Style and Finish	Price*
125A	49"	*Pomele*	7,140.
125A-BR	49"	Polished Ebony	7,740.
125A-BR	49"	Polished Walnut	7,980.
125A-BR	49"	Polished Mahogany	7,980.
125A-BR	49"	Open-pore Cherry	7,740.
125A-BR	49"	*Pomele*	8,280.
132	53"	Polished Ebony	7,540.
132	53"	Polished Walnut	8,300.
132	53"	Polished Mahogany	8,300.
132BR	53"	Polished Ebony	8,780.
132BR	53"	Polished Walnut	9,700.
132BR	53"	Polished Mahogany	9,700.

Grands

Model	Size	Style and Finish	Price*
156A-B	5' 3"	Ebony and Polished Ebony	19,940.
156A-B	5' 3"	Walnut and Polished Walnut	22,340.
156A-B	5' 3"	Mahogany and Polished Mahogany	22,340.
156A-B	5' 3"	Polished White	22,660.
156A-B	5' 3"	*Polished Pomele*	23,940.
156A-B	5' 3"	*Demi-Chip. Mahogany and Pol. Mahogany*	23,820.
156A-B	5' 3"	*Demi-Chip. Walnut and Polished Walnut*	23,820.
156A-B	5' 3"	*Chippendale Mahog. and Pol. Mahogany*	24,560.
156A-B	5' 3"	*Chippendale Walnut and Polished Walnut*	24,560.
156A-BR	5' 3"	Ebony and Polished Ebony	22,100.
156A-BR	5' 3"	Walnut and Polished Walnut	24,340.
156A-BR	5' 3"	Mahogany and Polished Mahogany	24,340.
156A-BR	5' 3"	Polished White	23,220.
156A-BR	5' 3"	*Polished Pomele*	25,940.
156A-BR	5' 3"	*Demi-Chip. Mahogany and Pol. Mahogany*	25,820.
156A-BR	5' 3"	*Demi-Chip. Walnut and Polished Walnut*	25,820.
156A-BR	5' 1"	*Chippendale Walnut and Polished Walnut*	26,560.
156A-BR	5' 1"	*Chippendale Mahog. and Pol. Mahogany*	26,560.
185A-B	6' 1"	Ebony and Polished Ebony	23,740.
185A-B	6' 1"	Walnut and Polished Walnut	26,360.
185A-B	6' 1"	Mahogany and Polished Mahogany	26,360.
185A-B	6' 1"	Polished White	26,500.
185A-B	6' 1"	*Empire Polished Ebony*	25,160.
185A-B	6' 1"	*Polished Vavone*	29,740.
185A-B	6' 1"	*Polished Pyramid Mahogany*	29,740.
185A-BR	6' 1"	Ebony and Polished Ebony	25,760.

*For explanation of terms and prices, please see pages 54–60.

Model	Size	Style and Finish	Price*

Bohemia (continued)

Model	Size	Style and Finish	Price*
185A-BR	6' 1"	Walnut and Polished Walnut	28,360.
185A-BR	6' 1"	Mahogany and Polished Mahogany	28,360.
185A-BR	6' 1"	Polished White	27,060.
185A-BR	6' 1"	*Empire Polished Ebony*	27,160.
185A-BR	6' 1"	*Polished Vavone*	31,740.
185A-BR	6' 1"	*Polished Pyramid Mahogany*	31,740.
225BR	7' 4"	*Polished Ebony*	37,940.
272R	8' 11"	*Polished Ebony*	47,940.

Bösendorfer

Verticals
130CL	*52"*	*Polished Ebony*	38,880.

Grands
170	5' 8"	Polished Ebony	79,980.
170	5' 8"	Polished, Satin, Open-pore: Walnut, Mahogany, Pomele, Cherry, Bubinga, Wenge, White	85,000.
170	5' 8"	Polished, Satin, Open-pore: Pyramid Mahogany, Amboyna, Rio Rosewood, Burl Walnut, Birdseye Maple, Yew, Macassar, Moor Oak	90,000.
170	5' 8"	"Johann Strauss" Polished Ebony	85,000.
170	5' 8"	"Johann Strauss," other finish	99,000.
170	5' 8"	"Franz Schubert" Polished Ebony	85,000.
170	5' 8"	"Franz Schubert," other finish	99,000.
170	5' 8"	"Vienna," any finish	103,000.
170	5' 8"	"Senator," any finish	93,000.
170	5' 8"	"Chopin," any finish	117,000.
170	5' 8"	"Classic" any finish	99,000.
170	5' 8"	"Yacht," any finish	99,000.
170	5' 8"	Chippendale, any finish	83,980.
170	5' 8"	Louis XV, any finish	99,980.
170	5' 8"	Baroque, any finish	99,980.
185	6' 1"	Polished Ebony	83,600.
185	6' 1"	Polished, Satin, Open-pore: Walnut, Mahogany, Pomele, Cherry, Bubinga, Wenge, White	90,600.
185	6' 1"	Polished, Satin, Open-pore: Pyramid	96,000.

Model	Size	Style and Finish	Price*
		Mahogany, Amboyna, Rio Rosewood, Burl Walnut, Birdseye Maple, Yew, Macassar, Moor Oak	
185	6' 1"	"Johann Strauss" Polished Ebony	90,600.
185	6' 1"	"Johann Strauss" other finish	105,600.
185	6' 1"	"Franz Schubert" Polished Ebony	90,600.
185	6' 1"	"Franz Schubert" other finish	105,600.
185	6' 1"	"Vienna," any finish	109,600.
185	6' 1"	"Senator," any finish	99,000.
185	6' 1"	"Chopin," any finish	119,800.
185	6' 1"	"Classic" any finish	105,600.
185	6' 1"	"Yacht," any finish	105,600.
185	6' 1"	"Porsche Design," any color	119,800.
185	6' 1"	Chippendale, any finish	87,600.
185	6' 1"	Louis XV, any finish	103,600.
185	6' 1"	Baroque, any finish	103,600.
200CS	6' 7"	"Conservatory" Ebony	65,200.
200	6' 7"	Polished Ebony	92,200.
200	6' 7"	Polished, Satin, Open-pore: Walnut, Mahogany, Pomele, Cherry, Bubinga, Wenge, White	100,600.
200	6' 7"	Polished, Satin, Open-pore: Pyramid Mahogany, Amboyna, Rio Rosewood, Burl Walnut, Birdseye Maple, Yew, Macassar, Moor Oak	105,200.
200	6' 7"	"Johann Strauss" Polished Ebony	100,600.
200	6' 7"	"Johann Strauss" other finish	115,800.
200	6' 7"	"Franz Schubert" Polished Ebony	100,600.
200	6' 7"	"Franz Schubert" other finish	115,800.
200	6' 7"	"Vienna," any finish	119,800.
200	6' 7"	"Senator," any finish	108,200.
200	6' 7"	"Chopin," any finish	130,000.
200	6' 7"	"Classic" any finish	115,800.
200	6' 7"	"Yacht," any finish	115,800.
200	6' 7"	Chippendale, any finish	96,200.
200	6' 7"	Louis XV, any finish	112,200.
200	6' 7"	Baroque, any finish	112,200.
214CS	7'	"Conservatory" Ebony	71,800.
214	7'	Polished Ebony	107,400.

*For explanation of terms and prices, please see pages 54–60.

Model	Size	Style and Finish	Price*

Bösendorfer (continued)

Model	Size	Style and Finish	Price*
214	7'	Polished, Satin, Open-pore: Walnut, Mahogany, Pomele, Cherry, Bubinga, Wenge, White	114,000.
214	7'	Polished, Satin, Open-pore: Pyramid Mahogany, Amboyna, Rio Rosewood, Burl Walnut, Birdseye Maple, Yew, Macassar, Moor Oak	118,000.
214	7'	"Johann Strauss" Polished Ebony	114,000.
214	7'	"Johann Strauss" other finish	130,000.
214	7'	"Franz Schubert" Polished Ebony	114,000.
214	7'	"Franz Schubert" other finish	130,000.
214	7'	"Vienna," any finish	134,000.
214	7'	"Senator," any finish	121,000.
214	7'	"Chopin," any finish	143,800.
214	7'	"Classic" any finish	130,000.
214	7'	"Yacht," any finish	130,000.
214	7'	"Porsche Design," any color	143,800.
214	7'	Chippendale, any finish	111,400.
214	7'	Louis XV, any finish	127,400.
214	7'	Baroque, any finish	127,400.
225	7' 4"	Polished Ebony	112,600.
225	7' 4"	Polished, Satin, Open-pore: Walnut, Mahogany, Pomele, Cherry, Bubinga, Wenge, White	122,600.
225	7' 4"	Polished, Satin, Open-pore: Pyramid Mahogany, Amboyna, Rio Rosewood, Burl Walnut, Birdseye Maple, Yew, Macassar, Moor Oak	127,800.
225	7' 4"	"Johann Strauss" Polished Ebony	122,600.
225	7' 4"	"Johann Strauss" other finish	140,600.
225	7' 4"	"Franz Schubert" Polished Ebony	122,600.
225	7' 4"	"Franz Schubert" other finish	140,600.
225	7' 4"	"Vienna," any finish	144,000.
225	7' 4"	"Senator," any finish	131,000.
225	7' 4"	"Chopin," any finish	149,800.
225	7' 4"	"Classic" any finish	140,600.
225	7' 4"	"Yacht," any finish	140,600.
225	7' 4"	Chippendale, any finish	116,600.
225	7' 4"	Louis XV, any finish	132,600.
225	7' 4"	Baroque, any finish	132,600.

Model	Size	Style and Finish	Price*
280	9' 2"	Polished Ebony	146,000.
280	9' 2"	Polished, Satin, Open-pore: Walnut, Mahogany, Pomele, Cherry, Bubinga, Wenge, White	156,600.
280	9' 2"	Polished, Satin, Open-pore: Pyramid Mahogany, Amboyna, Rio Rosewood, Burl Walnut, Birdseye Maple, Yew, Macassar, Moor Oak	162,600.
280	9' 2"	"Johann Strauss" Polished Ebony	156,600.
280	9' 2"	"Johann Strauss" other finish	178,000.
280	9' 2"	"Franz Schubert" Polished Ebony	156,600.
280	9' 2"	"Franz Schubert" other finish	178,000.
280	9' 2"	"Vienna," any finish	182,000.
280	9' 2"	"Senator," any finish	165,600.
280	9' 2"	"Chopin," any finish	191,600.
280	9' 2"	"Classic" any finish	178,000.
280	9' 2"	"Yacht," any finish	178,000.
280	9' 2"	"Porsche Design," any color	191,000.
280	9' 2"	Chippendale, any finish	151,000.
280	9' 2"	Louis XV, any finish	170,000.
280	9' 2"	Baroque, any finish	170,000.
290	9' 6"	Polished Ebony	166,000.
290	9' 6"	Polished, Satin, Open-pore: Walnut, Mahogany, Pomele, Cherry, Bubinga, Wenge, White	177,000.
290	9' 6"	Polished, Satin, Open-pore: Pyramid Mahogany, Amboyna, Rio Rosewood, Burl Walnut, Birdseye Maple, Yew, Macassar, Moor Oak	183,400.
290	9' 6"	"Johann Strauss" Polished Ebony	177,000.
290	9' 6"	"Johann Strauss" other finish	198,000.
290	9' 6"	"Franz Schubert" Polished Ebony	177,000.
290	9' 6"	"Franz Schubert" other finish	198,000.
290	9' 6"	"Vienna," any finish	202,000.
290	9' 6"	"Senator," any finish	186,400.
290	9' 6"	"Chopin," any finish	216,000.
290	9' 6"	"Classic" any finish	198,000.
290	9' 6"	"Yacht," any finish	198,000.
290	9' 6"	Chippendale, any finish	171,000.
290	9' 6"	Louis XV, any finish	190,000.
290	9' 6"	Baroque, any finish	190,000.

*For explanation of terms and prices, please see pages 54–60.

Model	Size	Style and Finish	Price*
Boston			
Verticals			
UP-118E	46"	Polished Ebony	9,440.
UP-118E	46"	Walnut	10,560.
UP-118E	46"	Polished Walnut	10,780.
UP-118E	46"	Polished Mahogany	10,780.
UP-118E	46"	Polished White	10,620.
UP-118A	46"	Art Deco Aniegre	7,990.
UP-118S	46"	Open-Pore Honey Oak	6,140.
UP-118S	46"	Open-Pore Black Oak	6,140.
UP-118S	46"	Open-Pore Red Oak	6,140.
UP-118S	46"	Mahogany	7,600.
UP-126E	50"	Polished Ebony	11,460.
UP-126E	50"	Polished Mahogany	13,220.
UP-132E	52"	Polished Ebony	12,580.
Grands			
GP-156	5' 1"	Ebony and Polished Ebony	16,520.
GP-163	5' 4"	Ebony	19,740.
GP-163	5' 4"	Polished Ebony	20,280.
GP-163	5' 4"	Mahogany	21,600.
GP-163	5' 4"	Polished Mahogany	22,200.
GP-163	5' 4"	Walnut	21,800.
GP-163	5' 4"	Polished Walnut	22,460.
GP-163	5' 4"	Polished White	20,840.
GP-163	5' 4"	Polished Ivory	20,840.
GP-178	5' 10"	Ebony	22,780.
GP-178	5' 10"	Polished Ebony	23,360.
GP-178	5' 10"	Mahogany	24,360.
GP-178	5' 10"	Polished Mahogany	25,020.
GP-178	5' 10"	Walnut	24,640.
GP-178	5' 10"	Polished Walnut	25,500.
GP-178	5' 10"	Polished White	23,860.
GP-178	5' 10"	Polished Ivory	23,860.
GP-193	6' 4"	Ebony	28,960.
GP-193	6' 4"	Polished Ebony	29,700.
GP-193	6' 4"	Walnut	32,260.
GP-193	6' 4"	Polished Mahogany	32,500.
GP-193	6' 4"	Polished White	31,260.
GP-218	7' 2"	Ebony	36,780.
GP-218	7' 2"	Polished Ebony	37,720.

Model	Size	Style and Finish	Price*

Breitmann

Verticals

Model	Size	Style and Finish	Price*
B110	44"	Polished Ebony	3,060.
B110	44"	Polished Mahogany	3,120.
B110	44"	Polished Brown Mahogany	3,120.
B120	48"	Polished Ebony	3,502.
B120	48"	Polished Mahogany	3,640.
B120	48"	Polished Brown Mahogany	3,640.
B122	49"	Polished Ebony	3,924.
B122	49"	Polished Mahogany	4,126.
B122	49"	Polished Brown Mahogany	4,126.
B130	52"	Polished Ebony	4,220.
B130	52"	Polished Mahogany	4,560.
B130	52"	Polished Brown Mahogany	4,560.
B130	52"	Polished White	4,320.

Grands

Model	Size	Style and Finish	Price*
B116	5' 2"	Polished Ebony	9,450.
B116	5' 2"	Polished White	9,600.

Cable, Hobart M.

Available finishes include: Ebony, Polished Ebony, Brown Mahogany, Polished Mahogany, Walnut, Polished Walnut, Brown Oak, Polished Red Oak, Cherry, Polished White, Polished Ivory.

Verticals

Model	Size	Style and Finish	Price*
UH 09	43"	Continental Polished Ebony	2,870.
UH 09	43"	Continental Cherry	2,910.
UH 09	43"	Continental Other Finishes	2,990.
UH 09L	43"	Continental (w/toe) Polished Ebony	2,950.
UH 09L	43"	Continental (w/toe) Brown Oak	2,990.
UH 09L	43"	Continental (w/toe) Walnut	2,990.
UH 09L	43"	Continental (w/toe) Cherry	2,990.
UH 09L	43"	Continental (w/toe) Other Finishes	3,070.
CH 12F	44"	French Provincial Cherry	3,370.
CH 12F	44"	French Provincial Brown Oak	3,370.
CH 12M	44"	Mediterranean Brown Oak	3,370.
CH 12M	44"	Mediterranean Cherry	3,370.
UH 12T	44"	Polished Ebony	3,080.
UH 12T	44"	Brown Oak	3,120.

*For explanation of terms and prices, please see pages 54–60.

Model	Size	Style and Finish	Price*

Cable, Hobart M. (continued)

Model	Size	Style and Finish	Price
UH 12T	44"	Walnut	3,120.
UH 12T	44"	Cherry	3,120.
UH 12T	44"	Other Finishes	3,200.
UH 16ST	45"	Polished Ebony (school)	3,160.
UH 16ST	45"	Brown Oak (school)	3,240.
UH 16ST	45"	Cherry (school)	3,240.
CH 19F	47"	French Provincial Cherry	3,700.
CH 19F	47"	French Provincial Brown Oak	3,700.
CH 19M	47"	Mediterranean Brown Oak	3,700.
CH 19M	47"	Mediterranean Cherry	3,700.
UH 19F	47"	Demi-Chippendale Polished Ebony	3,320.
UH 19F	47"	Demi-Chippendale Other Finishes	3,440.
UH 19ST	47"	Polished Ebony	3,200.
UH 19ST	47"	Brown Oak	3,240.
UH 19ST	47"	Cherry	3,240.
UH 19ST	47"	Other Finishes	3,320.
UH 19T	47"	Polished Ebony	3,200.
UH 19T	47"	Cherry	3,240.
UH 19T	47"	Other Finishes	3,320.
UH 22F	48"	Demi-Chippendale Polished Ebony	3,490.
UH 22F	48"	Demi-Chippendale Other Finishes	3,610.
UH 22T	48"	Polished Ebony	3,370.
UH 22T	48"	Other Finishes	3,490.
UH 32F	52"	French Provincial Polished Ebony	3,740.
UH 32F	52"	French Provincial Other Finishes	3,860.
UH 32T	52"	Polished Ebony	3,620.
UH 32T	52"	Other Finishes	3,740.

Grands

Model	Size	Style and Finish	Price
GH 42	4' 8"	Polished Ebony	8,420.
GH 42	4' 8"	Polished Ivory/White	8,620.
GH 42	4' 8"	Other Finishes	8,820.
GH 42F	4' 8"	French Provincial Polished Mahogany	9,420.
GH 42F	4' 8"	French Provincial Polished Walnut	9,420.
GH 42F	4' 8"	French Provincial Cherry	9,220.
GH 42F	4' 8"	French Provincial Polished Cherry	9,420.
GH 42F	4' 8"	French Provincial Brown Oak	9,220.
GH 52	5'	Polished Ebony	9,260.
GH 52	5'	Polished Ivory/White	9,460.
GH 52	5'	Other Finishes	9,660.

Model	Size	Style and Finish	Price*
GH 52F	5'	French Provincial Polished Ebony	9,860.
GH 52F	5'	French Provincial Polished Ivory/White	10,060.
GH 52F	5'	French Provincial Cherry	10,060.
GH 52F	5'	French Provincial Brown Oak	10,060.
GH 52F	5'	French Provincial Other Finishes	10,260.
GH 62	5' 4"	Polished Ebony	10,290.
GH 62	5' 4"	Polished Ivory/White	10,490.
GH 62	5' 4"	Other Finishes	10,690.
GH 62D	5' 4"	Bubinga	11,090.
GH 62D	5' 4"	Polished Birds-Eye Maple	13,710.
GH 62F	5' 4"	French Provincial Polished Ebony	10,890.
GH 62F	5' 4"	French Provincial Polished Ivory/White	11,090.
GH 62F	5' 4"	French Provincial Cherry	11,090.
GH 62F	5' 4"	French Provincial Brown Oak	11,090.
GH 62F	5' 4"	French Provincial Other Finishes	22,290.
GH 72	5' 8"	Polished Ebony	11,320.
GH 72	5' 8"	Polished Ivory/White	11,520.
GH 72	5' 8"	Polished Walnut	11,720.
GH 72	5' 8"	Polished Mahogany	11,720.
GH 72D	5' 8"	Bubinga	12,240.
GH 72D	5' 8"	Polished Bird's-Eye Maple	15,140.
GH 72F	5' 8"	French Provincial Polished Mahogany	11,920.
GH 72F	5' 8"	French Provincial Polished Walnut	12,320.
GH 87	6' 2"	Ebony	12,540.
GH 87	6' 2"	Polished Ebony	12,340.
GH 87	6' 2"	Polished Ivory/White	12,540.
GH 87	6' 2"	Walnut	12,540.
GH 87	6' 2"	Brown Oak	12,540.
GH 87	6' 2"	Brown Mahogany	12,540.
GH 87	6' 2"	Other Finishes	12,740.
GH 87F	6' 2"	French Provincial Polished Mahogany	13,340.
GH 87F	6' 2"	French Provincial Polished Walnut	13,340.
GH 87FFD	6' 2"	French Provincial Ivory & Gold	13,620.

Charles R. Walter — see "Walter, Charles R."

Chase, A. B.

Verticals

Model	Size	Style and Finish	Price
111	43"	Oak	3,190.
111	43"	Cherry	3,190.
111	43"	French Oak	3,190.
111	43"	French Cherry	3,190.
112	44"	Continental Polished Ebony	2,590.
112	44"	Continental Polished Mahogany	2,700.
113	45"	Polished Ebony	2,790.
113	45"	Polished Mahogany	2,900.
115CB	45"	Chippendale Polished Mahogany	3,100.
121	48"	Polished Ebony	3,190.
121	48"	Polished Mahogany	3,300.

Grands

Model	Size	Style and Finish	Price
152	5'	Polished Ebony	7,780.
152	5'	Polished Mahogany	8,280.
152	5'	Polished Sapeli Mahogany	8,280.
152	5'	Polished Walnut	8,280.
152	5'	Polished White	8,280.
165	5' 5"	Polished Ebony	8,780.
165	5' 5"	Polished Mahogany	9,280.
165	5' 5"	Polished Walnut	9,280.
185	6' 1"	Polished Ebony	10,580.
185	6' 1"	Polished Mahogany	11,180.

Conn

Verticals

Model	Size	Style and Finish	Price
C433	43"	French Cherry	2,790.
C434	43"	French Oak	2,790.
C435	43"	Oak	2,790.
C436	43"	Cherry	2,790.

Conover Cable

Verticals

Model	Size	Style and Finish	Price
CC-142	42"	Continental Polished Ebony	2,750.
CC-142	42"	Continental Polished Mahogany	2,850.
CC-142	42"	Continental Walnut	2,850.

Model	Size	Style and Finish	Price*
CC-142	42"	Continental Polished Walnut	2,850.
CC-142	42"	Continental Cherry	2,850.
CC-142	42"	Continental Polished Ivory/White	2,850.
CC-144F	44"	French Provincial Cherry	3,590.
CC-144M	44"	Mediterranean Brown Oak	3,390.
CC-144T	44"	Mahogany	3,590.
CC-145	45"	Ebony	3,050.
CC-145	45"	Polished Ebony	2,950.
CC-145	45"	Satin Wood Finishes	3,050.
CC-145	45"	Polished Mahogany	3,050.
CC-145	45"	Polished Ivory	3,050.
CC-118F	46-1/2"	French Provincial Cherry	4,190.
CC-118M	46-1/2"	Mediterranean Brown Oak	3,990.
CC-118T	46-1/2"	Mahogany	4,190.
CC-247	46-1/2"	Ebony and Polished Ebony	4,700.
CC-247	46-1/2"	Satin and Polished Wood Finishes	4,700.
CC-121F	48"	French Provincial Polished Ebony	4,100.
CC-121F	48"	French Provincial Polished Mahogany	4,300.
CC-121M	48"	Mediterranean Polished Ebony	3,990.
CC-121M	48"	Mediterranean Polished Mahogany	4,270.

Grands

Model	Size	Style and Finish	Price*
CCIG-50	4' 11-1/2"	Ebony	8,390.
CCIG-50	4' 11-1/2"	Polished Ebony	8,190.
CCIG-50	4' 11-1/2"	Polished Mahogany	8,790.
CCIG-50	4' 11-1/2"	Polished Walnut	8,790.
CCIG-50	4' 11-1/2"	Polished Ivory	8,790.
CCIG-54	5' 3"	Ebony	9,390.
CCIG-54	5' 3"	Polished Ebony	9,190.
CCIG-54	5' 3"	Polished Mahogany	9,790.
CCIG-54	5' 3"	Polished Walnut	9,790.
CCIG-54	5' 3"	Polished Ivory	9,790.
CCIG-54KBF	5' 3"	French Provincial Mahogany	10,990.
CCIG-54KBF	5' 3"	French Provincial Cherry	10,990.
CCIG-57	5' 7"	Ebony	10,190.
CCIG-57	5' 7"	Polished Ebony	9,990.
CCIG-57	5' 7"	Polished Mahogany	10,590.
CCIG-57	5' 7"	Polished Walnut	10,590.
CCIG-57	5' 7"	Polished Ivory	10,590.
CCIG-57L	5' 7"	Empire Ebony	10,990.

*For explanation of terms and prices, please see pages 54–60.

Model	Size	Style and Finish	Price*

Conover Cable (continued)

Model	Size	Style and Finish	Price*
CCIG-57L	5' 7"	Emprie Polished Ebony	10,790.
CCIG-57L	5' 7"	Empire Polished Mahogany	11,590.
CCIG-57L	5' 7"	Empire Polished Walnut	11,590.
CCIG-57L	5' 7"	Empire Polished Ivory	11,590.
CCIG-61	6' 1"	Ebony	10,990.
CCIG-61	6' 1"	Polished Ebony	10,790.
CCIG-61	6' 1"	Polished Mahogany	11,390.
CCIG-61	6' 1"	Polished Walnut	11,390.
CCIG-61	6' 1"	Polished Ivory	11,390.
CCIG-61L	6' 1"	Empire Ebony	11,790.
CCIG-61L	6' 1"	Empire Polished Ebony	11,590.
CCIG-61L	6' 1"	Empire Polished Mahogany	12,190.
CCIG-61L	6' 1"	Empire Polished Walnut	12,190.
CCIG-61L	6' 1"	Empire Polished Ivory	12,190.

Ebel, Carl

Verticals

Model	Size	Style and Finish	Price*
LF-109AB	43"	Continental Polished Ebony	4,180.
LF-109AC	43"	Continental Polished Mahogany	4,270.
LF-109AC	43"	Continental Polished Walnut	4,270.
LF-109AC	43"	Continental Polished White	4,270.
LF-109AF	43"	Continental Polished Ebony w/Molding	4,480.
LF-109AS	43"	Continental Cherry	4,270.
LF-109AS	43"	Continental Oak	4,270.
LF-109BB	43"	Polished Ebony (straight leg)	4,480.
LF-109BC	43"	Polished Mahogany (straight leg)	4,480.
LF-109BC	43"	Polished Walnut (straight leg)	4,480.
LF-109BC	43"	Polished White (straight leg)	4,480.
LF-109BF	43"	Pol. Mahogany w/Molding (straight leg)	4,630.
LF-109BF	43"	Pol. Walnut w/Molding (straight leg)	4,630.
LF-109BF	43"	Oak w/Molding (straight leg)	4,630.
LF-109EF	43"	Polished Ebony (curved leg)	4,630.
LF-109EF	43"	Polished Mahogany (curved leg)	4,780.
LF-109EF	43"	Polished Walnut (curved leg)	4,780.
LF-113G	44"	Queen Anne or Mediterranean Walnut	5,340.
LF-113G	44"	Queen Anne or Mediterranean Cherry	5,340.
LF-113G	44"	Queen Anne or Mediterranean Oak	5,340.
LM-115BB	45"	Polished Ebony	4,630.

Model	Size	Style and Finish	Price*
LM-115BC	45"	Polished Mahogany	4,780.
LM-115BC	45"	Walnut and Polished Walnut	4,780.
LM-115BC	45"	Oak	4,780.
LM-115BC	45"	Cherry	4,780.
LM-115BF	45"	Polished Ebony with Molding	4,990.
LM-115BF	45"	Polished Mahogany with Molding	4,990.
LM-115BF	45"	Polished Walnut with Molding	4,990.
LM-115G	45"	Walnut	4,930.
LM-115G	45"	Cherry	4,930.
LM-115G	45"	Oak	4,930.
LM-116EF	46"	Chippendale Polished Ebony	4,780.
LM-116EF	46"	Chippendale Pol. Mahogany w/Molding	4,990.
LM-116EF	46"	Chippendale Pol. Walnut w/Molding	4,990.
LM-116H	46"	Polished Ebony (straight leg)	4,780.
LM-116H	46"	Polished Mahogany (straight leg)	5,090.
LM-116H	46"	Polished Walnut (straight leg)	5,090.
LM-116H	46"	Polished Oak (straight leg)	5,090.
LM-116H	46"	Polished White (straight leg)	5,090.
LM-116H	46"	Pol. Ebony w/Mahog. or Walnut Accents	4,780.
LM-117CW	46"	Walnut	5,980.
LM-117GW	46"	Walnut (curved leg)	5,980.
LT-122BB	48"	Polished Ebony (straight leg)	5,530.
LT-122BC	48"	Polished Mahogany (straight leg)	5,830.
LT-122BC	48"	Polished Walnut (straight leg)	5,830.
LT-122BC	48"	Polished White (straight leg)	5,830.
LT-122BF	48"	Polished Ebony w/Molding (straight leg)	5,980.
LT-122BF	48"	Pol. Mahogany w/Molding (straight leg)	5,980.
LT-122BF	48"	Polished Walnut w/Molding (straight leg)	5,980.
LT-125GW	49"	Walnut	6,280.
LT-125GW	49"	Cherry	6,280.
LT-125GW	49"	Oak	6,280.

Grands

Model	Size	Style and Finish	Price*
F-150BB	4' 11"	Polished Ebony	9,990.
F-150BC	4' 11"	Polished Mahogany	10,490.
F-150BC	4' 11"	Polished Walnut	10,490.
F-150BC	4' 11"	Polished White	10,490.
F-158BB	5' 2"	Polished Ebony	14,380.
F-158BC	5' 2"	Polished Mahogany	14,980.
F-158BC	5' 2"	Polished Walnut	14,980.

*For explanation of terms and prices, please see pages 54–60.

Model	Size	Style and Finish	Price*

Ebel, Carl (continued)

Model	Size	Style and Finish	Price*
F-158BC	5' 2"	Polished Oak	14,980.
F-158BC	5' 2"	Polished White	14,980.
F-158BC	5' 2"	Polished Ivory	14,980.
F-158BS	5' 2"	Walnut	14,980.
F-158CB	5' 2"	Polished Ebony (round leg)	15,580.
F-158CC	5' 2"	Polished Mahogany (round leg)	15,580.
F-158CC	5' 2"	Polished Walnut (round leg)	15,580.
F-158E	5' 2"	Polished Ebony (French leg)	15,880.
F-158E	5' 2"	Polished Mahogany (French leg)	15,880.
F-158E	5' 2"	Polished Walnut (French leg)	15,880.
F-185BB	6' 1"	Polished Ebony	16,480.
F-185BC	6' 1"	Polished Mahogany	17,380.
F-185BC	6' 1"	Walnut and Polished Walnut	17,380.
F-185BC	6' 1"	Polished White	17,380.
F-185BC	6' 1"	Polished Ivory	17,380.
F-185CC	6' 1"	Polished Mahogany (round leg)	17,980.
F-185CC	6' 1"	Polished Walnut (round leg)	17,980.
F-185E	6' 1"	Polished Ebony (French leg)	17,980.
F-185E	6' 1"	Polished Mahogany (French leg)	17,980.
F-185E	6' 1"	Polished Walnut (French leg)	17,980.

Essex

Verticals

Model	Size	Style and Finish	Price*
EUP-107C	42"	Continental Polished Ebony	5,190.
EUP-111E	44"	European Polished Ebony	5,750.
EUP-111E	44"	European Polished Mahogany	5,890.
EUP-111E	44"	European Polished Walnut	5,950.
EUP-111E	44"	European Polished White	5,790.
EUP-111F	44"	European Cherry	6,270.
EUP-111M	44"	Modern Walnut	5,990.
EUP-111R	44"	English Regency Mahogany	5,830.
EUP-111T	44"	Ash	5,870.

Grands

Model	Size	Style and Finish	Price*
EGP-161	5' 3"	Ebony	14,060.
EGP-161	5' 3"	Polished Ebony	13,790.
EGP-161	5' 3"	Mahogany	15,180.
EGP-161	5' 3"	Polished Mahogany	14,900.

Model	Size	Style and Finish	Price*
EGP-161	5' 3"	Walnut	15,580.
EGP-161	5' 3"	Cherry	15,820.
EGP-161	5' 3"	Oak	15,500.
EGP-161	5' 3"	Polished White	13,960.
EGP-161N	5' 3"	Neo-Classic Mahogany	17,700.
EGP-161N	5' 3"	Neo-Classic Polished Mahogany	17,500.
EGP-161N	5' 3"	Neo-Classic Cherry	18,500.
EGP-183	6'	Ebony	18,100.
EGP-183	6'	Polished Ebony	17,840.
EGP-183	6'	Polished Mahogany	19,050.
EGP-183	6'	Walnut	19,850.

Estonia

Prices include Jansen adjustable artist bench.

Grands

168	5' 6"	Ebony and Polished Ebony	23,700.
168	5' 6"	Mahogany and Polished Mahogany	26,000.
168	5' 6"	Walnut and Polished Walnut	26,000.
168	5' 6"	African Bubinga and Pol. African Bubinga	28,000.
168	5' 6"	"Hidden Beauty" Pol. Ebony w/Bubinga	26,500.
190	6' 3"	Ebony and Polished Ebony	29,300.
190	6' 3"	Mahogany and Polished Mahogany	31,900.
190	6' 3"	Walnut and Polished Walnut	31,900.
190	6' 3"	African Bubinga and Pol. African Bubinga	34,000.
190	6' 3"	"Hidden Beauty" Pol. Ebony w/Bubinga	31,300.
273	9'	Ebony and Polished Ebony	71,000.

Everett

Verticals

EV-111F	43"	French Provincial Cherry	3,190.
EV-111F	43"	French Provincial Oak	3,190.
EV-111T	43"	Cherry	3,190.
EV-111T	43"	Oak	3,190.
EV-112	44"	Continental Polished Ebony	2,590.
EV-112	44"	Continental Polished Mahogany	2,700.

*For explanation of terms and prices, please see pages 54–60.

Model	Size	Style and Finish	Price*

Everett (continued)

Model	Size	Style and Finish	Price*
EV-113	45"	Polished Ebony	2,790.
EV-113	45"	Polished Mahogany	2,900.
EV-115CB	45"	Chippendale Polished Mahogany	3,100.
EV-121	48"	Polished Ebony	3,190.
EV-121	48"	Polished Mahogany	3,300.

Grands

Model	Size	Style and Finish	Price*
EV-152	5'	Polished Ebony	7,780.
EV-152	5'	Polished Mahogany	8,280.
EV-152	5'	Polished Sapeli Mahogany	8,480.
EV-152	5'	Polished Walnut	8,280.
EV-152	5'	Polished White	8,280.
EV-165	5' 5"	Polished Ebony	8,780.
EV-165	5' 5"	Polished Mahogany	9,280.
EV-165	5' 5"	Polished Walnut	9,280.
EV-174	5' 8"	Polished Ebony	9,380.
EV-185	6' 1"	Polished Ebony	10,780.
EV-185	6' 1"	Polished Mahogany	11,380.

Falcone

Available finishes include: Ebony, Polished Ebony, Brown Mahogany, Polished Mahogany, Walnut, Polished Walnut, Brown Oak, Polished Red Oak, Cherry, Polished White, Polished Ivory.

Verticals

Model	Size	Style and Finish	Price*
CF 12FD	44"	French Provincial Brown Oak	3,490.
CF 12FD	44"	French Provincial Cherry	3,490.
CF 12MD	44"	Mediterranean Brown Oak	3,490.
CF 12MD	44"	Mediterranean Cherry	3,490.
UF 12T	44"	Polished Ebony	3,080.
UF 12T	44"	Brown Oak	3,120.
UF 12T	44"	Walnut	3,120.
UF 12T	44"	Cherry	3,120.
UF 12T	44"	Other Finishes	3,200.
CF 13FD	45"	French Provincial Cherry	3,650.
CF 13MD	45"	Mahogany	3,650.
CF 13MD	45"	Cherry	3,650.
CF 19FD	47"	French Provincial Brown Oak	3,820.
CF 19FD	47"	French Provincial Cherry	3,820.

Model	Size	Style and Finish	Price*
CF 19MD	47"	Mediterranean Brown Oak	3,820.
CF 19MD	47"	Mediterranean Cherry	3,820.
CF 19QA	47"	Queen Anne Brown Oak	3,920.
CF 19QA	47"	Queen Anne Cherry	3,920.
CF 19QA	47"	Queen Anne Mahogany	3,920.
UF 19F	47"	Demi-Chippendale Polished Ebony	3,320.
UF 19F	47"	Demi-Chippendale Other Finishes	3,440.
UF 19T	47"	Polished Ebony	3,200.
UF 19T	47"	Cherry	3,240.
UF 19T	47"	Other Finishes	3,320.
UF 20T	47"	Polished Ebony	3,490.
UF 20T	47"	Other Finishes	3,610.
UF 23FD	48"	French Provincial Polished Ebony	3,740.
UF 23FD	48"	French Provincial Other Finishes	3,860.
UF 23TD	48"	Polished Ebony	3,620.
UF 23TD	48"	Other Finishes	3,740.
UF 26T	52"	Polished Ebony	3,840.
UF 26T	52"	Polished Mahogany	3,960.
UF 32F	52"	French Provincial Polished Ebony	3,740.
UF 32F	52"	French Provincial Other Finishes	3,860.
UF 32T	52"	Polished Ebony	3,620.
UF 32T	52"	Other Finishes	3,740.

Grands

Model	Size	Style and Finish	Price*
GF 42D	4' 8"	Polished Ebony	8,540.
GF 42D	4' 8"	Polished Ivory	8,740.
GF 42D	4' 8"	Walnut	8,940.
GF 52D	5'	Polished Ebony	9,380.
GF 52D	5'	Polished Ivory/White	9,580.
GF 52D	5'	Other Finishes	9,780.
GF 52FD	5'	French Polished Ebony	9,980.
GF 52FD	5'	French Polished Ivory/White	10,180.
GF 52FD	5'	French Cherry	10,180.
GF 52FD	5'	French Brown Oak	10,180.
GF 52FD	5'	French Other Finishes	10,380.
GF 62D	5' 4"	Polished Ebony	10,410.
GF 62D	5' 4"	Polished Ivory/White	10,610.
GF 62D	5' 4"	Other Finishes	10,810.
GF 62D	5' 4"	Bubinga	11,210.
GF 62D	5' 4"	Polished Bird's-Eye Maple	13,710.
GF 62FD	5' 4"	French Provincial Polished Ebony	11,010.

*For explanation of terms and prices, please see pages 54–60.

Model	Size	Style and Finish	Price*

Falcone (continued)

Model	Size	Style and Finish	Price*
GF 62FD	5' 4"	French Provincial Polished Ivory/White	11,210.
GF 62FD	5' 4"	French Provincial Cherry	11,210.
GF 62FD	5' 4"	French Provincial Brown Oak	11,210.
GF 62FD	5' 4"	French Provincial Other Finishes	11,410.
GF 72D	5' 8"	Polished Ebony	11,440.
GF 72D	5' 8"	Polished Ivory/White	11,640.
GF 72D	5' 8"	Polished Mahogany	11,840.
GF 72D	5' 8"	Polished Walnut	11,840.
GF 72D	5' 8"	Bubinga	12,240.
GF 72D	5' 8"	Polished Bird's-Eye Maple	15,140.
GF 72FD	5' 8"	French Provincial Polished Mahogany	12,440.
GF 72FD	5' 8"	French Provincial Polished Walnut	12,440.
GF 72FD	5' 8"	French Provincial Polished Ivory/White	12,240.
GF 87D	6' 2"	Polished Ebony	12,460.
GF 87D	6' 2"	Polished Ivory/White	12,660.
GF 87D	6' 2"	Polished Brown Mahogany	12,660.
GF 87D	6' 2"	Polished Brown Oak	12,660.
GF 87D	6' 2"	Walnut	12,660.
GF 87D	6' 2"	Other Finishes	12,860.
GF 87FFD	6' 2"	French Provincial Ivory & Gold	13,620.

Fazioli

Fazioli is willing to make custom-designed cases with exotic veneers, marquetry, and other embellishments. Prices on request to Fazioli.

Grands

Model	Size	Style and Finish	Price*
F156	5' 2"	Ebony and Polished Ebony	81,700.
F156	5' 2"	Walnut	85,560.
F156	5' 2"	Polished Walnut	87,680.
F156	5' 2"	Polished Pyramid Mahogany	90,450.
F156	5' 2"	Cherry	85,560.
F156	5' 2"	Polished Cherry	87,680.
F183	6'	Ebony and Polished Ebony	92,680.
F183	6'	Walnut	97,760.
F183	6'	Polished Walnut	99,740.
F183	6'	Polished Pyramid Mahogany	103,240.
F183	6'	Cherry	97,760.
F183	6'	Polished Cherry	99,740.
F212	6' 11"	Ebony and Polished Ebony	106,100.

Model	Size	Style and Finish	Price*
F212	6' 11"	Walnut	111,400.
F212	6' 11"	Polished Walnut	113,880.
F212	6' 11"	Polished Pyramid Mahogany	117,720.
F212	6' 11"	Cherry	111,400.
F212	6' 11"	Polished Cherry	113,880.
F228	7' 6"	Ebony and Polished Ebony	120,860.
F228	7' 6"	Walnut	126,800.
F228	7' 6"	Polished Walnut	128,900.
F228	7' 6"	Polished Pyramid Mahogany	134,890.
F228	7' 6"	Cherry	126,800.
F228	7' 6"	Polished Cherry	128,900.
F278	9' 2"	Ebony and Polished Ebony	154,540.
F278	9' 2"	Walnut	162,250.
F278	9' 2"	Polished Walnut	165,980.
F278	9' 2"	Polished Pyramid Mahogany	171,600.
F278	9' 2"	Cherry	162,250.
F278	9' 2"	Polished Cherry	165,980.
F308	10' 2"	Ebony and Polished Ebony	192,000.
F308	10' 2"	Walnut	200,100.
F308	10' 2"	Polished Walnut	201,560.
F308	10' 2"	Polished Pyramid Mahogany	210,440.
F308	10' 2"	Cherry	200,100.
F308	10' 2"	Polished Cherry	201,560.
All models		*Fourth Pedal, add'l*	8,800.
All models		*Third and Fourth Pedals (set), add'l*	10,400.
All models		*Magnetic Balanced Action, add'l*	11,800.

Feurich

Prices do not include bench.

Verticals

Model	Size	Style and Finish	Price*
F 123	49"	Polished Ebony	26,130.
F 123	49"	Polished Mahogany	29,930.

Grands

Model	Size	Style and Finish	Price*
F 172	5' 8"	Polished Ebony	65,320.
F 172 ADF	5' 8"	"Old German Style" Polished Ebony	79,222.
F 172 ADF	5' 8"	"Old German Style" Cherry	79,390.
F 172	5' 8"	Rococo	107,110.
F 227	7' 5"	Polished Ebony	97,240.
F 227 ADF	7' 5"	"Old German Style" Polished Ebony	106,480.

*For explanation of terms and prices, please see pages 54–60.

Förster, August

Prices do not include bench.

Verticals

Model	Size	Style and Finish	Price
116C	46"	Chippendale Polished Ebony	18,544.
116C	46"	Chippendale Walnut and Polished Walnut	19,426.
116C	46"	Chippendale Mahog. and Pol. Mahogany	18,619.
116C	46"	Chippendale Polished White	18,960.
116D	46"	Continental Polished Ebony	15,721.
116D	46"	Continental Walnut and Polished Walnut	16,666.
116D	46"	Continental Mahog.and Pol. Mahogany	15,772.
116D	46"	Continental Polished White	16,150.
116E	46"	Polished Ebony	18,544.
116E	46"	Walnut and Polished Walnut	19,426.
116E	46"	Mahogany and Polished Mahogany	18,619.
116E	46"	Polished White	18,960.
125G	49"	Polished Ebony	19,917.
125G	49"	Walnut and Polished Walnut	20,887.
125G	49"	Mahogany and Polished Mahogany	19,980.
125G	49"	Polished White	20,346.

Grands

Model	Size	Style and Finish	Price
170	5' 8"	Polished Ebony	40,918.
170	5' 8"	Walnut and Polished Walnut	42,367.
170	5' 8"	Mahogany and Polished Mahogany	40,994.
170	5' 8"	Polished White	42,695.
170	5' 8"	*Pyramid Mahogany*	46,714.
170	5' 8"	"Classic" Polished Ebony	45,668.
170	5' 8"	"Classic" Walnut and Polished Walnut	51,880.
170	5' 8"	"Classic" Mahogany and Pol. Mahogany	46,525.
170	5' 8"	"Classic" Polished White	49,221.
170	5' 8"	*Chippendale, additional*	9,513.
190	6' 4"	Polished Ebony	46,386.
190	6' 4"	Walnut and Polished Walnut	47,949.
190	6' 4"	Mahogany and Polished Mahogany	46,550.
190	6' 4"	Polished White	48,226.
190	6' 4"	*Pyramid Mahogany*	52,182.
190	6' 4"	"Classic" Polished Ebony	51,137.
190	6' 4"	"Classic" Walnut and Polished Walnut	57,462.
190	6' 4"	"Classic" Mahogany and Pol.Mahogany	52,082.
190	6' 4"	"Classic" Polished White	54,753.

Model	Size	Style and Finish	Price*
190	6' 4"	*Chippendale, additional*	9,513.
215	7' 2"	Polished Ebony	53,140.
275	9' 1"	Polished Ebony	100,440.

Grotrian

Prices do not include bench.

Verticals

Caprice	42-1/2"	Polished Ebony	15,197.
Fried. Grotrian	44"	Polished Ebony	12,861.
Carat	45-1/2"	Polished Ebony	18,662.
College	48"	Polished Ebony	20,590.
Classic	49"	Polished Ebony	24,403.
Concertino	52"	Polished Ebony	28,619.

Grands

Chambre	5' 5"	Polished Ebony	46,782.
Cabinet	6' 3"	Polished Ebony	53,528.
Concert	7' 4"	Polished Ebony	63,051.
Concert Royal	9' 1"	Polished Ebony	76,256.

Haessler

Prices do not include bench.

Verticals

115 K	45"	Ebony and Polished Ebony	13,180.
115 K	45"	Waxed Alder	12,918.
115 K	45"	Beech	12,918.
115 K	45"	Ash	12,918.
115 K	45"	White and Polished White	13,774.
118 K	47"	Ebony and Polished Ebony	14,744.
118 K	47"	Ebony with Walnut Accent	15,954.
118 K	47"	Mahogany and Polished Mahogany	15,536.
118 K	47"	Walnut and Polished Walnut	15,536.
118 K	47"	Cherry and Polished Cherry	15,976.
118 K	47"	Cherry with Yew Inlay, Satin and Polish	16,856.
118 K	47"	Oak	13,930.
118 K	47"	White and Polished White	15,360.
118 KM	47"	Ebony and Polished Ebony	15,624.
118 KM	47"	White and Polished White	16,284.

*For explanation of terms and prices, please see pages 54–60.

Haessler (continued)

Model	Size	Style and Finish	Price*
118 CH	47"	Chippendale Mahogany and Pol.Mahogany	16,856.
118 CH	47"	Chippendale Walnut and Polished Walnut	17,230.
124 K	49"	Ebony and Polished Ebony	15,800.
124 K	49"	Ebony with Walnut Accent	16,702.
124 K	49"	Mahogany and Polished Mahogany	17,120.
124 K	49"	Walnut and Polished Walnut	17,120.
124 K	49"	Cherry and Polished Cherry	17,626.
124 K	49"	Cherry with Yew Inlay, Satin and Polish	18,506.
124 K	49"	White and Polished White	16,460.
124 KM	49"	Ebony and Polished Ebony	16,414.
124 KM	49"	White and Polished White	16,414.
132	52"	Ebony and Polished Ebony	22,242.

Grands

Model	Size	Style and Finish	Price*
175	5' 8"	Ebony and Polished Ebony	46,630.
175	5' 8"	Mahogany and Polished Mahogany	48,495.
175	5' 8"	Walnut and Polished Walnut	48,963.
175	5' 8"	Cherry and Polished Cherry	48,728.
175	5' 8"	Polished Bubinga	51,293.
175	5' 8"	White and Polished White	48,963.
175	5' 8"	Saxony Polished Pyramid Mahogany	61,524.
175	5' 8"	Saxony Polished Burl Walnut	62,115.
175	5' 8"	"President" Polished Ebony	52,059.
175	5' 8"	"President" Polished Mahogany	54,141.
175	5' 8"	"President" Polished Walnut	54,662.
175	5' 8"	"President" Polished Bubinga	57,266.
175	5' 8"	Louis XV, Satin and Polished	54,427.
175	5' 8"	Louis XV Mahogany, Satin and Polished	57,147.
175	5' 8"	Louis XV Walnut, Satin and Polished	56,602.
175	5' 8"	Kaiser Wilhelm II Polished Ebony	54,898.
175	5' 8"	Kaiser Wilhelm II Polished Mahogany	57,093.
175	5' 8"	Kaiser Wilhelm II Polished Walnut	57,645.
175	5' 8"	Kaiser Wilhelm II Polished Cherry	57,369.
175	5' 8"	Ambassador East Indian Rosewood	63,892.
175	5' 8"	Ambassador Walnut	59,159.
175	5' 8"	Nicolas II Walnut w/Burl Inlay	63,892.
175	5' 8"	Louis XVI Rococo White w/Gold	68,624.
175	5' 8"	Classic Alexandra Polished Ebony	53,005.
175	5' 8"	Classic Alexandra Polished Mahogany	55,655.
175	5' 8"	Classic Alexandra Polished Walnut	55,124.

Model	Size	Style and Finish	Price*
186	6' 1"	Ebony and Polished Ebony	52,536.
186	6' 1"	Mahogany and Polished Mahogany	54,310.
186	6' 1"	Walnut and Polished Walnut	55,164.
186	6' 1"	Cherry and Polished Cherry	54,899.
186	6' 1"	Polished Bubinga	57,802.
186	6' 1"	White and Polished White	55,164.
186	6' 1"	Saxony Polished Pyramid Mahogany	69,318.
186	6' 1"	Saxony Polished Burl Walnut	69,983.
186	6' 1"	"President" Polished Ebony	58,654.
186	6' 1"	"President" Polished Mahogany	60,999.
186	6' 1"	"President" Polished Walnut	61,587.
186	6' 1"	"President" Polished Bubinga	64,519.
186	6' 1"	Louis XV, Satin and Polished	61,318.
186	6' 1"	Louis XV Mahogany, Satin and Polished	64,383.
186	6' 1"	Louis XV Walnut, Satin and Polished	63,772.
186	6' 1"	Kaiser Wilhelm II Polished Ebony	61,853.
186	6' 1"	Kaiser Wilhelm II Polished Mahogany	64,327.
186	6' 1"	Kaiser Wilhelm II Polished Walnut	64,945.
186	6' 1"	Kaiser Wilhelm II Polished Cherry	64,636.
186	6' 1"	Ambassador East Indian Rosewood	71,982.
186	6' 1"	Ambassador Walnut	66,652.
186	6' 1"	Nicolas II Walnut w/Burl Inlay	71,982.
186	6' 1"	Louis XVI Rococo White w/Gold	77,316.
186	6' 1"	Classic Alexandra Polished Ebony	59,720.
186	6' 1"	Classic Alexandra Polished Mahogany	62,706.
186	6' 1"	Classic Alexandra Polished Walnut	62,108.

Hallet, Davis & Co.

Verticals

H-C43F	43"	French Oak	2,990.
H-C43F	43"	French Mahogany	2,990.
H-C43F	43"	French Cherry	2,990.
H-C43F	43"	French Walnut	2,990.
H-C43R	43"	Oak (round leg)	2,990.
H-C43R	43"	Mahogany (round leg)	2,990.
H-C43S	43"	Italian Provincial Walnut	2,990.
H-C43S	43"	Italian Provincial Mahogany	2,990.
H-C43S	43"	Italian Provincial Cherry	2,990.

*For explanation of terms and prices, please see pages 54–60.

Hallet, Davis & Co. (continued)

Model	Size	Style and Finish	Price*
H-111GD	44"	Continental Polished Ebony	2,500.
H-111GD	44"	Continental Polished Mahogany	2,550.
H-111GD	44"	Continental Polished Walnut	2,550.
H-111GD	44"	Continental Polished White	2,550.
H-115GC	45"	Chippendale Polished Ebony	2,750.
H-115GC	45"	Chippendale Polished Mahogany	2,790.
H-115WH	46"	Polished Ebony	2,790.
H-115WH	46"	Polished Mahogany	2,840.
H-115WH	46"	Polished Walnut	2,840.
H-121WH	48"	Polished Ebony	2,990.
H-121WH	48"	Polished Mahogany	3,100.
H-121WH	48"	Polished Walnut	3,100.
H-126	50"	Polished Ebony	3,590.
H-126	50"	Polished Mahogany	3,700.

Grands

Model	Size	Style and Finish	Price*
H-143	4' 8"	Polished Ebony	6,390.
H-143	4' 8"	Polished Mahogany	6,790.
H-143	4' 8"	Polished Walnut	6,790.
H-143F	4' 8"	Queen Anne Polished Ebony	7,190.
H-143F	4' 8"	Queen Anne Polished Mahogany	7,190.
H-143F	4' 8"	Queen Anne Polished Walnut	7,190.
H-152C	5'	Ebony	8,390.
H-152C	5'	Polished Ebony	7,990.
H-152C	5'	Mahogany	8,590.
H-152C	5'	Polished Mahogany	8,390.
H-152C	5'	Polished Walnut	8,390.
H-152C	5'	Polished White	8,390.
H-152D	5'	Polished Ebony	8,590.
H-152D	5'	Mahogany	9,190.
H-152D	5'	Polished Mahogany	8,990.
H-152D	5'	Polished Walnut	8,990.
H-152S	5'	Queen Anne Polished Ebony	8,590.
H-152S	5'	Queen Anne Mahogany	9,190.
H-152S	5'	Queen Anne Polished Mahogany	8,990.
H-165C	5' 5"	Ebony	9,190.
H-165C	5' 5"	Polished Ebony	8,790.
H-165C	5' 5"	Mahogany	9,390.
H-165C	5' 5"	Polished Mahogany	9,190.
H-165C	5' 5"	Polished Walnut	9,190.

Model	Size	Style and Finish	Price*
H-165C	5' 5"	Polished White	9,190.
H-165D	5' 5"	Polished Mahogany	9,790.
H-185C	6' 1"	Polished Ebony	10,790.
H-185C	6' 1"	Polished Mahogany	11,190.
H-185C	6' 1"	Polished Walnut	11,190.
H-215C	7' 1"	Polished Ebony	16,990.

Hamilton

Verticals

Model	Size	Style and Finish	Price*
H100	39"	Continental Polished Ebony (73-note)	1,978.
H100	39"	Continental Polished Cherry (73-note)	2,098.
H350	42-1/2"	Continental Polished Ebony	2,790.
H350	42-1/2"	Continental Polished Mahogany	2,790.
H310	43"	Vintage Mahogany	2,990.
H310	43"	American Oak	2,990.
H310	43"	Hallmark Cherry	2,990.
H360	47"	Classic Polished Ebony	3,390.
H360	47"	Classic Polished Mahogany	3,390.

Grands

Model	Size	Style and Finish	Price*
H391	4' 7"	Polished Ebony	7,750.
H391	4' 7"	Polished Mahogany	7,950.
H391	4' 7"	Polished White	7,750.
H396	5' 1"	Polished Ebony	8,990.
H396	5' 1"	Polished Mahogany	9,290.
H396	5' 1"	Polished White	8,990.
H399	5' 8"	Ebony	10,798.
H399	5' 8"	Polished Ebony	10,398.
H399	5' 8"	Polished Mahogany	10,798.

*For explanation of terms and prices, please see pages 54–60.

Model	Size	Style and Finish	Price*

Hayden

Verticals

Model	Size	Style and Finish	Price*
UP-110GD	43"	Cherry	2,990.
UP-110GE	43"	Mahogany	3,190.
114RPN	45"	Polished Dark Walnut	3,190.
115FM	45-1/2"	Mahogany	3,190.
115OS	45-1/2"	Light Cherry	3,190.
115GC	45-1/2"	Polished Mahogany	3,390.
121RP	48"	Polished Ebony	3,390.

Grands

Model	Size	Style and Finish	Price*
G-152	5'	Polished Ebony	7,790.
G-165	5' 6"	Polished Ebony	8,790.
G-185	6' 1"	Polished Ebony	10,580.

Hyundai

Verticals

Model	Size	Style and Finish	Price*
U-800	42"	Continental Polished Ebony	3,998.
U-800	42"	Continental Walnut	3,758.
U-800	42"	Continental Polished Mahogany	4,300.
U-800	42"	Continental Polished White	4,300.
U-800	42"	Continental Polished Ivory	3,998.
U-824F	43"	French Walnut	4,998.
U-824F	43"	French Brown Oak	4,998.
U-824F	43"	French Cherry	4,998.
U-824M	43"	Mediterranean Brown Oak	4,998.
U-824M	43"	Mediterranean Walnut	4,998.
U-824M	43"	Mediterranean Cherry	4,998.
U-842	46"	Chippendale Polished Mahogany	5,598.
U-852	46"	Ebony and Polished Ebony	5,598.
U-852	46"	Brown Oak	5,598.
U-852	46"	Walnut	5,198.
U-860E	46"	Cherry	5,398.
U-860E	46"	Walnut	5,398.
U-832	48"	Ebony and Polished Ebony	5,198.
U-832	48"	Walnut and Polished Walnut	5,398.
U-832	48"	Brown Oak	5,398.
U-832	48"	Polished Mahogany	5,398.
U-837	52"	Ebony	5,598.

Model	Size	Style and Finish	Price*
U-837	52"	Polished Ebony	5,698.
U-837	52"	Walnut	5,598.
U-837	52"	Polished Walnut	5,798.
U-837	52"	Polished Mahogany	5,798.

Grands

Model	Size	Style and Finish	Price*
G-50A	4' 7"	Ebony	9,898.
G-50A	4' 7"	Polished Ebony	9,998.
G-50A	4' 7"	Walnut and Polished Walnut	10,398.
G-50A	4' 7"	Polished Mahogany	10,398.
G-50A	4' 7"	Brown Oak and Polished Brown Oak	10,398.
G-50A	4' 7"	Cherry	10,398.
G-50A	4' 7"	Polished Ivory	10,198.
G-50A	4' 7"	Polished White	10,198.
G-50AF	4' 7"	Queen Anne Walnut and Pol. Walnut	11,900.
G-50AF	4' 7"	Queen Anne Polished Mahogany	11,900.
G-50AF	4' 7"	Queen Anne Oak and Polished Oak	11,900.
G-50AF	4' 7"	Queen Anne Cherry	11,900.
G-50AF	4' 7"	Queen Anne Polished White	11,900.
G-50AF	4' 7"	Queen Anne Polished Ivory	11,900.
G-80A	5' 1"	Ebony	11,398.
G-80A	5' 1"	Polished Ebony	11,498.
G-80A	5' 1"	Walnut and Polished Walnut	11,898.
G-80A	5' 1"	Polished Mahogany	11,898.
G-80A	5' 1"	Brown Oak and Polished Brown Oak	11,898.
G-80A	5' 1"	Cherry	11,898.
G-80A	5' 1"	Polished Ivory	11,698.
G-80A	5' 1"	Polished White	11,698.
G-80AF	5' 1"	Queen Anne Polished Mahogany	14,098.
G-80B	5' 1"	Chippendale Polished Mahogany	14,098.
G-81	5' 9"	Chippendale Polished Mahogany	15,398.
G-82	5' 9"	Ebony	12,798.
G-82	5' 9"	Polished Ebony	12,898.
G-82	5' 9"	Walnut and Polished Walnut	13,298.
G-82	5' 9"	Polished Mahogany	13,298.
G-82	5' 9"	Polished White	13,098.
G-82AF	5' 9"	Queen Anne Polished Mahogany	15,398.
G-84	6' 1"	Ebony	13,498.
G-84	6' 1"	Polished Ebony	13,598.
G-84	6' 1"	Walnut and Polished Walnut	13,998.
G-84	6' 1"	Polished Mahogany	13,998.
G-85	6' 10"	Ebony and Polished Ebony	17,398.

*For explanation of terms and prices, please see pages 54–60.

Ibach

Verticals

Model	Size	Style and Finish	Price*
B-114	45"	"Classic/Tradition" Open-Pore Beech	16,754.
B-114	45"	"Classic/Tradition" Open-Pore Alder	16,754.
B-114	45"	"Classic/Tradition" Open-Pore Oak	16,754.
B-114	45"	"Classic/Tradition" Open-Pore Maple	17,115.
B-114	45"	"Classic/Tradition" Open-Pore Cherry	17,115.
C-118	46-1/2"	"Elegance" Open-Pore Beech	18,054.
C-118	46-1/2"	"Elegance" Open-Pore Oak	18,054.
C-118	46-1/2"	"Elegance" Open-Pore Cherry	18,460.
C-118	46-1/2"	"Elegance" Polished Ebony	18,517.
C-118	46-1/2"	"Elegance" Polished White	19,155.
C-118	46-1/2"	"Elegance" Polished Walnut	19,910.
C-118	46-1/2"	"Elegance" Polished Mahogany	19,910.
C-118	46-1/2"	"Elegance" Polished Cherry	19,910.
C-118	46-1/2"	"Elegance" Polished Burr Walnut	22,057.
C-118	46-1/2"	"Edition (Bruno Paul 1911)" Pol. Ebony	21,651.
C-118	46-1/2"	"Edition (Bruno Paul 1911)" Pol. White	22,436.
C-118	46-1/2"	"Edition (Bruno Paul1911)" Oiled Oak	22,436.
C-118	46-1/2"	"Antik" Polished Ebony	on request
K-125	49"	"Exclusive" Polished Ebony	on request
H-128	50"	"Edition" Swiss Pear-Tree	on request
L-132	52"	"Tradition" Polished Ebony	26,060.

Grands

Model	Size	Style and Finish	Price*
F-II 183	6'	Polished Ebony	53,731.
F-II 183	6'	Polished Mahogany	59,474.
F-II 183	6'	Polished Burr Walnut	60,912.
F-II 183	6'	*"Edition Ibach Design 1913"*	56,318.
F-II 183	6'	*"Eigenentwurf Ibach Design 1908"*	55,680.
F-II 183	6'	*"Ausfuhrung Art Design"*	66,873.
F-III 215	7' 1"	"Richard Strauss" Polished Ebony	68,064.
F-III 215	7' 1"	*"Klassizismus"*	115,767.
F-III 215	7' 1"	*"Richard Meier"*	on request
F-IV 240	7' 10-1/2"	"Richard Wagner" Polished Ebony	74,168.

Model	Size	Style and Finish	Price*

Irmler

Verticals

Model	Size	Style and Finish	Price*
M113E	44"	Polished Ebony	7,323.
M113E	44"	Walnut	7,082.
M113E	44"	Polished Walnut	7,435.
M113E	44"	Mahogany	7,259.
M113E	44"	Polished Mahogany	7,435.
M113E	44"	Cherry	7,259.
M113E	44"	Polished Cherry	7,435.
M113E	44"	Beech	7,082.
M113E	44"	Alder	7,082.
M113E	44"	Polished White	7,792.
M122E	49"	Polished Ebony	7,832.
M122E	49"	Walnut	7,616.
M122E	49"	Polished Walnut	7,792.
M122E	49"	Mahogany	7,792.
M122E	49"	Polished Mahogany	7,969.
M122E	49"	Cherry	7,792.
M122E	49"	Polished Cherry	7,969.
M122E	49"	Polished Cherry with Inlay	8,658.
M122E	49"	Polished Bubinga	9,351.
M122E	49"	Beech	7,435.
M122E	49"	Alder	7,435.
M122E	49"	Polished White	8,322.

Grands

Model	Size	Style and Finish	Price*
F16E	5' 7"	Polished Ebony	26,194.
F16E	5' 7"	Walnut	27,143.
F16E	5' 7"	Polished Walnut	27,787.
F16E	5' 7"	Mahogany	27,143.
F16E	5' 7"	Polished Mahogany	27,787.
F16E	5' 7"	Cherry	26,347.
F16E	5' 7"	Polished Cherry	28,400.
F16E	5' 7"	Polished White	26,837.
F18E	5' 11"	Polished Ebony	28,093.
F18E	5' 11"	Walnut	29,043.
F18E	5' 11"	Polished Walnut	29,656.
F18E	5' 11"	Mahogany	29,043.
F18E	5' 11"	Polished Mahogany	29,656.
F18E	5' 11"	Cherry	28,400.

*For explanation of terms and prices, please see pages 54–60.

Model	Size	Style and Finish	Price*

Irmler (continued)

Model	Size	Style and Finish	Price*
F18E	5' 11"	Polished Cherry	30,299.
F18E	5' 11"	Polished White	29,380.
F18E	5' 11"	"Classic" Polished Ebony	33,148.
F18E	5' 11"	"Classic" Polished Walnut	34,404.
F18E	5' 11"	"Classic" Polished Mahogany	34,404.
F18E	5' 11"	"Classic" Polished Cherry	35,048.
F18E	5' 11"	Chippendale Polished Ebony	33,148.
F18E	5' 11"	Chippendale Polished Walnut	34,711
F18E	5' 11"	Chippendale Polished Mahogany	34,711.
F18E	5' 11"	Chippendale Polished White	34,711.
F122E	7' 3"	Polished Ebony	41,359.
F122E	7' 3"	Polished Walnut	44,422.
F122E	7' 3"	Polished Mahogany	44,422.
F122E	7' 3"	Polished Cherry	44,422.
F122E	7' 3"	Polished White	42,890.

Kawai

Verticals

Model	Size	Style and Finish	Price*
K-18	44-1/2"	Polished Ebony	4,730.
K-18	44-1/2"	Polished Mahogany	5,330.
506N	44-1/2"	Mahogany	3,590.
506N	44-1/2"	Oak	3,590.
508	44-1/2"	Mahogany	4,190.
508	44-1/2"	Oak	4,190.
606	44-1/2"	American Oak	4,490.
606	44-1/2"	French Renaissance Cherry	4,690.
606	44-1/2"	Queen Anne Mahogany	4,790.
606	45"	Queen Anne Cherry	5,990.
606	45"	Spanish Provincial Oak	5,890.
608	44-1/2"	Classic Spanish Oak	5,090.
608	44-1/2"	French Provincial Cherry	5,190.
608	44-1/2"	Queen Anne Mahogany	5,190.
UST-7	46"	Ebony	6,690.
UST-7	46"	Oak	6,690.
UST-7	46"	Walnut	6,690.
UST-8	46"	Ebony	5,590.
UST-8	46"	Walnut	5,590.
UST-8	46"	Oak	5,590.

Model	Size	Style and Finish	Price*
VT-118	46"	Vari-Touch Oak	6,190.
906	46-1/2"	Country Manor Oak	7,090.
906	46-1/2"	English Regency Mahogany	7,190.
906	46-1/2"	French Provincial Cherry	7,190.
UST-10	48"	Ebony	7,990.
UST-10	48"	Mahogany	7,990.
K-25	48"	Ebony and Polished Ebony	5,790.
K-25	48"	Mahogany and Polished Mahogany	6,390.
K-25	48"	Polished Snow White	6,190.
K-50	49"	Ebony and Polished Ebony	7,990.
K-50	49"	Polished Sapeli Mahogany	9,290.
K-50	49"	Walnut	8,890.
K-50	49"	Polished Walnut	9,290.
UST-12	52"	Ebony	9,990.
UST-12	52"	Mahogany	9,990.
K-60	52"	Ebony and Polished Ebony	10,790.
VT-132	52"	Vari-Touch Polished Ebony	11,590.
K-80	52"	Ebony and Polished Ebony	12,990.

Grands

Model	Size	Style and Finish	Price*
GM-10C	5'	Polished Ebony	9,990.
GM-10LE	5'	Ebony	12,290.
GM-10LE	5'	Polished Ebony	12,390.
GM-10LE	5'	Polished Mahogany	13,590.
GM-10LE	5'	Polished Snow White	13,590.
GM-10LE	5'	French Provincial Polished Mahogany	14,590.
GE-20	5' 1"	Ebony	14,490.
GE-20	5' 1"	Polished Ebony	14,890.
GE-20	5' 1"	Walnut	16,390.
GE-20	5' 1"	Mahogany	16,190.
GE-20	5' 1"	Polished Mahogany	16,590.
GE-20	5' 1"	Polished Sapeli Mahogany	16,590.
GE-20	5' 1"	Polished Snow White	15,990.
GE-20	5' 1"	French Provincial Polished Mahogany	17,990.
GE-20C	5' 1"	Conservatory Polished Ebony	14,890.
GE-30	5' 5"	Ebony and Polished Ebony	16,990.
GE-30	5' 5"	Mahogany	18,890.
GE-30	5' 5"	Polished Mahogany	18,990.
GE-30	5' 5"	Polished Sapeli Mahogany	18,890.
GE-30	5' 5"	Polished Snow White	18,190.

*For explanation of terms and prices, please see pages 54–60.

Model	Size	Style and Finish	Price*

Kawai (continued)

Model	Size	Style and Finish	Price*
GE-30C	5' 5"	Conservatory Polished Ebony	16,990.
RX-1	5' 5"	Ebony and Polished Ebony	19,990.
RX-1	5' 5"	Walnut	21,390.
RX-1	5' 5"	Polished Walnut	21,990.
RX-1	5' 5"	Polished Sapeli Mahogany	21,590.
RX-1	5' 5"	Polished Snow White	20,790.
RX-2	5' 10"	Ebony and Polished Ebony	22,690.
RX-2	5' 10"	Walnut	24,390.
RX-2	5' 10"	Polished Walnut	25,590.
RX-2	5' 10"	Polished Mahogany	24,390.
RX-2	5' 10"	Polished Sapeli Mahogany	24,590.
RX-2	5' 10"	Oak	23,390.
RX-2	5' 10"	Cherry	24,390.
RX-2	5' 10"	Polished Rosewood	28,990.
RX-2	5' 10"	Polished Snow White	23,790.
RX-2	5' 10"	French Provincial Polished Mahogany	28,790.
RX-3	6' 1"	Ebony and Polished Ebony	29,390.
RX-3	6' 1"	Walnut	31,590.
RX-3	6' 1"	Polished Sapeli Mahogany	32,190.
RX-3	6' 1"	Polished Snow White	30,390.
CR40N	6' 1"	Plexiglass	75,260.
RX-5	6' 6"	Ebony and Polished Ebony	32,790.
RX-5	6' 6"	Walnut	35,690.
RX-5	6' 6"	Polished Sapeli Mahogany	35,690.
RX-5	6' 6"	Polished Snow White	34,190.
RX-6	7'	Ebony and Polished Ebony	36,790.
RX-7	7' 6"	Ebony and Polished Ebony	42,190.
GS-100	9' 1"	Polished Ebony	79,990.
EX	9' 1"	Polished Ebony	109,190.
EX-G	9' 1"	Polished Ebony	115,990.

Kawai, Shigeru

Grands

Model	Size	Style and Finish	Price*
SK2	5' 10"	Polished Ebony	34,900.
SK2	5' 10"	Polished Sapeli Mahogany	36,900.
SK2	5' 10"	Polished Pyramid Mahogany	55,900.
SK2	5' 10"	"Classic Noblesse" w/Burl Walnut Inlay	54,900.
SK3	6' 1"	Polished Ebony	40,900.

Model	Size	Style and Finish	Price*
SK3	6' 1"	Polished Sapeli Mahogany	42,900.
SK5	6' 6"	Polished Ebony	46,900.
SK5	6' 6"	Polished Sapeli Mahogany	49,900.
SK6	7'	Polished Ebony	52,900.
SK6	7'	Polished Sapeli Mahogany	57,900.
SK6	7'	*"Classic Noblesse" w/Burl Walnut Inlay*	77,900.
SK7	7' 6"	Polished Ebony	58,900.
SK7	7' 6"	Polished Sapeli Mahogany	63,900.
SK7	7' 6"	*"Classic Noblesse" w/Burl Walnut Inlay*	82,900.

Kemble

Verticals

Cambridge	43"	Mahogany	7,040.
Cambridge	43"	Walnut	7,040.
Oxford	43"	Mahogany	7,240.
Oxford	43"	Walnut	7,240.
Classic-T	45"	Polished Ebony	8,400.
Classic-T	45"	Polished Ebony and Chrome	8,700.
Empire	46-1/2"	Empire Polished Mahogany	10,240.
Prestige	46-1/2"	Cherry with Yew Inlay	10,240.
Windsor	46-1/2"	Polished Ebony with Burr Walnut	9,340.
Windsor	46-1/2"	Polished Mahogany	9,140.
K121ZT	48"	Polished Ebony	10,240.
K121ZT	48"	Georgian Mahogany Lustre	9,990.
K121ZT	48"	Polished Mahogany	10,240.
Vermont	48"	Cherry	11,940.
Quantum II	49"	Polished Ebony	11,940.
K131	52"	Polished Ebony	13,640.
K131	52"	Polished Mahogany	13,640.
K131	52"	Walnut	12,740.
K131	52"	Polished Walnut	13,640.

Grands

KC 173	5' 8"	Polished Ebony	24,990.

*For explanation of terms and prices, please see pages 54–60.

Klima

Price does not include bench.

Verticals

Model	Size	Style and Finish	Price
K-115	45-1/2"	Continental Polished Ebony	8,272.
K-115	45-1/2"	Continental Polished Mahogany	8,572.
K-115	45-1/2"	Continental Walnut	8,188.
K-115	45-1/2"	Continental Polished Oak	8,092.
K-115	45-1/2"	Continental Polished White	8,488.
K-117	47"	Polished Ebony	8,404.
K-117	47"	Polished Mahogany	8,704.
K-117	47"	Walnut	8,308.
K-117	47"	Oak	8,224.
K-117	47"	Polished White	8,608.
K-125	49"	Polished Ebony	8,632.
K-125	49"	Polished Mahogany	8,956.

Grands

Model	Size	Style and Finish	Price
K-195	6' 3"	Polished Ebony	54,216.

Knabe, Wm.

Verticals

Model	Size	Style and Finish	Price
WKV-118F	46-1/2"	French Provincial Polished Mahogany	6,190.
WKV-118F	46-1/2"	French Provincial Polished Cherry	6,190.
WKV-118R	46-1/2"	Renaissance Ebony and Polished Ebony	6,190.
WKV-118R	46-1/2"	Renaissance Polished Walnut	6,190.
WKV-118R	46-1/2"	Renaissance Oak	5,990.
WKV-118T	46-1/2"	Polished Mahogany	6,190.
WKV-118T	46-1/2"	Polished Walnut	6,190.
WKV-118T	46-1/2"	Polished Cherry	6,190.
WKV-121D	48"	Ebony	6,390.
WKV-121D	48"	Polished Ebony	6,190.
WKV-131MD	52"	Ebony	6,990.
WKV-131MD	52"	Polished Ebony	6,790.

Grands

Model	Size	Style and Finish	Price
WKG-53	5' 3"	Ebony and Polished Ebony	15,990.
WKG-53	5' 3"	Semi-Gloss Mahogany	16,590.
WKG-53	5' 3"	Semi-Gloss Walnut	16,590.
WKG-53	5' 3"	Semi-Gloss Cherry	16,590.
WKG-53KBF	5' 3"	French Provincial Semi-Gloss Mahogany	18,590.
WKG-53KBF	5' 3"	French Provincial Semi-Gloss Walnut	18,590.

Model	Size	Style and Finish	Price*
WKG-53KBF	5' 3"	French Provincial Semi-Gloss Cherry	18,590.
WKG-53M	5' 3"	Empire Ebony and Polished Ebony	17,190.
WKG-53M	5' 3"	Empire Semi-Gloss Mahogany	17,790.
WKG-53M	5' 3"	Empire Semi-Gloss Walnut	17,790.
WKG-53M	5' 3"	Empire Semi-Gloss Cherry	17,790.
WKG-57	5' 7"	Ebony and Polished Ebony	21,990.
WKG-57	5' 7"	Semi-Gloss Mahogany	23,990.
WKG-57	5' 7"	Semi-Gloss Walnut	23,990.
WKG-57	5' 7"	Semi-Gloss Cherry	23,990.
WKG-58	5' 8"	Ebony and Polished Ebony	22,990.
WKG-58	5' 8"	Semi-Gloss Mahogany	24,990.
WKG-58	5' 8"	Semi-Gloss Walnut	24,990.
WKG-58	5' 8"	Semi-Gloss Cherry	24,990.
WKG-58F	5' 8"	Louis XV Ebony and Polished Ebony	24,990.
WKG-58F	5' 8"	Louis XV Semi-Gloss Mahogany	26,990.
WKG-58F	5' 8"	Louis XV Semi-Gloss Walnut	26,990.
WKG-58M	5' 8"	Empire Ebony and Polished Ebony	24,190.
WKG-58M	5' 8"	Empire Semi-Gloss Mahogany	26,190.
WKG-58M	5' 8"	Empire Semi-Gloss Walnut	26,190.
WKG-58M	5' 8"	Empire Semi-Gloss Cherry	26,190.
WKG-61	6' 1"	Ebony and Polished Ebony	22,990.
WKG-61	6' 1"	Semi-Gloss Mahogany	24,990.
WKG-61	6' 1"	Semi-Gloss Walnut	24,990.
WKG-61	6' 1"	Semi-Gloss Cherry	24,990.
WKG-61L	6' 1"	Empire Semi-Gloss Mahogany	26,190.
WKG-61L	6' 1"	Empire Semi-Gloss Walnut	26,190.
WKG-61L	6' 1"	Empire Semi-Gloss Cherry	26,190.
WKG-64	6' 4"	Ebony	26,900.
WKG-64	6' 4"	Semi-Gloss Mahogany	28,900.
WKG-64	6' 4"	Semi-Gloss Walnut	28,900.
WKG-64F	6' 4"	Ebony	28,900.
WKG-64F	6' 4"	Semi-Gloss Mahogany	30,900.
WKG-64F	6' 4"	Semi-Gloss Walnut	30,900.
WKG-64M	6' 4"	Ebony	28,100.
WKG-64M	6' 4"	Semi-Gloss Mahogany	30,100.
WKG-64M	6' 4"	Semi-Gloss Walnut	30,100.
WKG-68	6' 8"	Ebony and Polished Walnut	22,990.
WKG-68	6' 8"	Semi-Gloss Mahogany	24,990.
WKG-68	6' 8"	Semi-Gloss Walnut	24,990.
WKG-68	6' 8"	Semi-Gloss Cherry	24,990.
WKG-70	7'	Ebony and Polished Ebony	28,000.

*For explanation of terms and prices, please see pages 54–60.

Kohler & Campbell

Verticals

Model	Size	Style and Finish	Price
KC-142	42"	Continental Polished Ebony	2,750.
KC-142	42"	Continental Polished Mahogany	2,850.
KC-142	42"	Continental Polished Walnut	2,850.
KC-142	42"	Continental Cherry	2,850.
KC-142	42"	Continental Polished Ivory	2,850.
KC-244F	44"	French Provincial Cherry	3,590.
KC-244M	44"	Mediterranean Brown Oak	3,390.
KC-244T	44"	Mahogany	3,590.
KC-245	45"	Polished Ebony	2,950.
KC-245	45"	Polished Mahogany	3,050.
KC-245	45"	Polished Walnut	3,050.
KC-245	45"	Cherry	3,050.
KC-245	45"	Polished Ivory	3,050.
KC-247	46-1/2"	Ebony and Polished Ebony	4,700.
KC-247	46-1/2"	Satin/Polished Wood Finishes	4,700.
KC-647F	46-1/2"	French Provincial Cherry	4,190.
KC-647R	46-1/2"	Renaissance Walnut	3,990.
KC-647T	46-1/2"	Mahogany	4,190.
KMV-47F	46-1/2"	French Provincial Semi-gloss Cherry	5,790.
KMV-47F	46-1/2"	French Provincial Semi-gloss Mahogany	5,790.
KMV-47T	46-1/2"	Semi-gloss Cherry	5,790.
KMV-47T	46-1/2"	Semi-gloss Mahogany	5,790.
KMV-47T	46-1/2"	American Oak	5,790.
KC-121F	48"	French Provincial Polished Ebony	4,190.
KC-121F	48"	French Provincial Polished Mahogany	4,390.
KC-121M	48"	Mediterranean Polished Ebony	3,990.
KC-121M	48"	Mediterranean Polished Mahogany	4,270.
KMV-48SD	48"	Ebony	7,390.
KMV-48SD	48"	Polished Ebony	5,990.
KMV-48SD	48"	Polished Mahogany	7,390.
KMV-52MD	52"	Ebony	7,790.
KMV-52MD	52"	Polished Ebony	6,390.
KMV-52MD	52"	Polished Mahogany	7,790.

Grands

Model	Size	Style and Finish	Price
KCG-450	4' 9"	Ebony	8,390.
KCG-450	4' 9"	Polished Ebony	8,190.
KCG-450	4' 9"	Polished Mahogany	8,790.

Model	Size	Style and Finish	Price*
KCG-450	4' 9"	Polished Walnut	8,790.
KCG-450	4' 9"	Polished Ivory	8,790.
KCG-450KBF	4' 9"	French Provincial Polished Mahogany	9,990.
KCG-450KBF	4' 9"	French Provincial Polished Cherry	9,990.
KCG-500	5' 1-1/2"	Ebony	9,790.
KCG-500	5' 1-1/2"	Polished Ebony	9,590.
KCG-500	5' 1-1/2"	Polished Mahogany	10,190.
KCG-500	5' 1-1/2"	Polished Walnut	10,190.
KCG-500	5' 1-1/2"	Polished Ivory	10,190.
KCG-500KBF	5' 1-1/2"	French Provincial Polished Mahogany	11,390.
KCG-500KBF	5' 1-1/2"	French Provincial Polished Cherry	11,390.
SKG-530S	5' 2"	Ebony	11,990.
SKG-530S	5' 2"	Polished Ebony	11,590.
SKG-530S	5' 2"	Polished Mahogany	12,990.
SKG-530S	5' 2"	Polished Walnut	12,990.
SKG-530S	5' 2"	Polished Ivory	12,990.
KFM-530A	5' 2"	Ebony	13,390.
KFM-530A	5' 2"	Polished Ebony	12,990.
KFM-530A	5' 2"	Polished Mahogany	14,390.
KFM-530A	5' 2"	Polished Walnut	14,390.
KFM-530A	5' 2"	Polished Ivory	14,390.
KFM-530AM	5' 2"	Empire Ebony	14,590.
KFM-530AM	5' 2"	Empire Polished Ebony	14,190.
KFM-530AM	5' 2"	Empire Polished Mahogany	15,590.
KFM-530AM	5' 2"	Empire Polished Walnut	15,590.
KFM-530AM	5' 2"	Empire Polished Ivory	15,590.
KFM-530AKBF	5' 2"	French Provincial Polished Mahogany	16,390.
KFM-530AKBF	5' 2"	French Provincial Polished Walnut	16,390.
KFM-530AKBF	5' 2"	French Provincial Polished Ivory	16,390.
KCG-600	5' 9"	Ebony	10,590.
KCG-600	5' 9"	Polished Ebony	10,390.
KCG-600	5' 9"	Polished Mahogany	10,990.
KCG-600	5' 9"	Polished Walnut	10,990.
KCG-600	5' 9"	Polished Ivory	10,990.
KCG-600L	5' 9"	Empire Ebony	11,390.
KCG-600L	5' 9"	Empire Polished Ebony	11,190.
KCG-600L	5' 9"	Empire Polished Mahogany	11,790.
KCG-600L	5' 9"	Empire Polished Walnut	11,790.
KCG-600L	5' 9"	Empire Polished Ivory	11,790.
KFM-600A	5' 9"	Ebony	17,390.
KFM-600A	5' 9"	Polished Ebony	15,990.

*For explanation of terms and prices, please see pages 54–60.

Model	Size	Style and Finish	Price*

Kohler & Campbell (continued)

Model	Size	Style and Finish	Price*
KFM-600A	5' 9"	Polished Mahogany	16,390.
KFM-600A	5' 9"	Polished Walnut	16,390.
KFM-600A	5' 9"	Polished Ivory	16,390.
KFM-600AM	5' 9"	Ebony	17,590.
KFM-600AM	5' 9"	Polished Ebony	17,190.
KFM-600AM	5' 9"	Polished Mahogany	18,590.
KFM-600AM	5' 9"	Polished Walnut	18,590.
KFM-600AM	5' 9"	Polished Ivory	18,590.
KCG-650	6' 1"	Ebony	11,390.
KCG-650	6' 1"	Polished Ebony	11,190.
KCG-650	6' 1"	Polished Mahogany	11,790.
KCG-650	6' 1"	Polished Walnut	11,790.
KCG-650	6' 1"	Polished Ivory	11,790.
KCG-650L	6' 1"	Empire Ebony	12,190.
KCG-650L	6' 1"	Empire Polished Ebony	11,990.
KCG-650L	6' 1"	Empire Polished Mahogany	12,590.
KCG-650L	6' 1"	Empire Polished Walnut	12,590.
KCG-650L	6' 1"	Empire Polished Ivory	12,590.
KFM-650A	6' 1"	Ebony	17,590.
KFM-650A	6' 1"	Polished Ebony	17,190.
KFM-650A	6' 1"	Polished Mahogany	18,590.
KFM-650A	6' 1"	Polished Walnut	18,590.
KFM-650A	6' 1"	Polished Ivory	18,590.
KFM-650AM	6' 1"	Empire Ebony	18,790.
KFM-650AM	6' 1"	Empire Polished Ebony	18,390.
KFM-650AM	6' 1"	Empire Polished Mahogany	19,790.
KFM-650AM	6' 1"	Empire Polished Walnut	19,790.
KFM-650AM	6' 1"	Empire Polished Ivory	19,790.
KFM-700A	6' 8"	Ebony	23,600.
KFM-700A	6' 8"	Polished Ebony	23,000.
KFM-700A	6' 8"	Polished Mahogany	25,000.
KFM-700A	6' 8"	Polished Walnut	25,000.
KFM-700A	6' 8"	Polished Ivory	25,000.
KFM-850A	7' 4"	Ebony	28,500.
KFM-850A	7' 4"	Polished Ebony	27,900.

Krakauer

Verticals

Model	Size	Style and Finish	Price*
K443	44"	French Cherry	3,190.
K444	44"	French Oak	3,190.
K445	44"	Oak	3,190.
K446	44"	Cherry	3,190.
K110B	44"	Polished Ebony	3,190.
K110R	44"	Polished Mahogany	3,190.
K110T	44"	Polished Walnut	3,190.
K110W	44"	Polished White	3,190.
K120B	48"	Polished Ebony	3,390.
K120R	48"	Polished Mahogany	3,390.
K120T	48"	Polished Walnut	3,390.
K120W	48"	Polished White	3,390.
K122	48-3/4"	*Polished Ebony*	3,500.
K122	48-3/4"	*Polished Mahogany*	3,500.
K122	48-3/4"	*Polished Walnut*	3,500.
K122	48-3/4"	*Polished White*	3,500.
K125	50"	*Polished Ebony*	3,590.
K125	50"	*Polished Mahogany*	3,590.
K125	50"	*Polished Walnut*	3,590.
K125	50"	*Polished White*	3,590.

Grands

Model	Size	Style and Finish	Price*
KG-155	5' 1"	Polished Ebony	7,590.

Mason & Hamlin

Verticals

Model	Size	Style and Finish	Price*
50	50"	Polished Ebony	17,862.

Grands

Model	Size	Style and Finish	Price*
A	5' 8"	Ebony	45,368.
A	5' 8"	Polished Ebony	48,516.
A	5' 8"	Mahogany	48,780.
A	5' 8"	Polished Pyramid Mahogany	59,298.
A	5' 8"	Walnut	48,780.
A	5' 8"	Rosewood	54,144.
A	5' 8"	Bubinga	54,144.
A	5' 8"	Polished Bubinga	56,038.

*For explanation of terms and prices, please see pages 54–60.

Model	Size	Style and Finish	Price*

Mason & Hamlin (continued)

Model	Size	Style and Finish	Price*
A	5' 8"	Macassar Ebony	57,292.
A	5' 8"	Polished Macassar Ebony	59,298.
A	5' 8"	"Monticello" Polished Ebony	51,682.
A	5' 8"	"Monticello" Mahogany	51,930.
A	5' 8"	"Monticello" Rosewood	62,954.
AA	6' 4"	Ebony	52,344.
AA	6' 4"	Polished Ebony	54,042.
AA	6' 4"	Mahogany	55,100.
BB	7'	Ebony	59,322.
BB	7'	Polished Ebony	61,028.
BB	7'	Mahogany	61,422.
BB	7'	Polished Pyramid Mahogany	73,130.
BB	7'	Walnut	61,422.
BB	7'	Rosewood	68,758.
BB	7'	Bubinga	68,758.
BB	7'	Polished Bubinga	70,464.
BB	7'	Macassar Ebony	71,360.
BB	7'	Polished Macassar Ebony	73,130.
BB	7'	"Monticello" Polished Ebony	63,942.
BB	7'	"Monticello" Mahogany	64,572.
BB	7'	"Monticello" Rosewood	79,246.

McPhail

Verticals

Size	Style and Finish	Price
44"	Console w/toeblock Ebony Polish/Satin	3,190.
44"	Console w/toeblock Mahogany	3,289.
44"	Console w/toeblock Furniture Cabinet	3,454.
47"	Studio w/toeblock Ebony Polish/Satin	3,738.
47"	Studio w/toeblock Mahogany	3,888.
47"	Studio w/toeblock Furniture Cabinet	4,288.

Grands

Size	Style and Finish	Price
5'	Ebony and Polished Ebony	8,327.
5'	Mahogany	8,723.
5' 4"	Ebony and Polished Ebony	9,280.
5' 4"	Mahogany	9,825.

Miller, Henry F.

Verticals

Model	Size	Style and Finish	Price
HMV-043	42-1/2"	Continental Polished Ebony	3,200.
HMV-043	42-1/2"	Continental Polished Mahogany	3,350.
HMV-045	43"	French Provincial Polished Cherry	4,220.
HMV-045	43"	Polished Oak	4,220.
HMV-045	43"	Polished Cherry	4,220.
HMV-047	46"	Polished Ebony	3,800.
HMV-047	46"	Polished Mahogany	4,000.
HMV-048	48"	Cherry	4,720.

Grands

Model	Size	Style and Finish	Price
HMG-056	4' 7"	Polished Ebony	9,070.
HMG-056	4' 7"	Polished Mahogany	9,120.
HMG-056F	4' 7"	French Provincial Cherry	9,920.
HMG-063	5' 3"	Ebony	10,530.
HMG-063	5' 3"	Polished Ebony	10,330.
HMG-063	5' 3"	Polished Mahogany	10,730.
HMG-063F	5' 3"	French Provincial Cherry	11,730.
HMG-072	6'	Ebony	14,340.
HMG-072	6'	Polished Ebony	14,140.
HMG-072	6'	Polished Mahogany	14,540.

Niendorf

Prices do not include bench.

Grands

Model	Size	Style and Finish	Price
145	4' 9"	Polished Ebony	28,192.
145	4' 9"	Polished Dark Mahogany	28,192.
145	4' 9"	Polished Medium Walnut	28,192.
145	4' 9"	Chippendale Polished Ebony	29,150.
145	4' 9"	Chippendale Polished Dark Mahogany	29,150.
145	4' 9"	Chippendale Polished Medium Walnut	29,150.
182	6'	Polished Ebony	32,854.
182	6'	Polished Dark Mahogany	32,854.
182	6'	Polished Medium Walnut	32,854.

*For explanation of terms and prices, please see pages 54–60.

Model	Size	Style and Finish	Price*

Nordiska

Verticals

Model	Size	Style and Finish	Price*
109-CM	43"	Continental Polished Ebony	2,480.
109-CM	43"	Continental Polished Mahogany	2,480.
114-MC	45"	French Walnut	3,580.
114-MC	45"	French Mahogany	3,580.
114-MCH	45"	Walnut	3,580.
114-MCH	45"	Mahogany	3,580.
116-CB	46"	Chippendale Polished Ebony	3,580.
116-CB	46"	Chippendale Polished Walnut	3,580.
116-CB	46"	Chippendale Polished Mahogany	3,580.
118-C GT	48"	Polished Ebony	3,480.
118-MC	48"	Walnut	3,780.
118-MC	48"	Mahogany	3,780.
118-MC	48"	Oak	3,780.
120-CA	48"	Polished Ebony	3,780.
120-CA	48"	Polished Mahogany	3,780.
126-Pro	50"	Polished Ebony	4,580.
126-Pro	50"	Walnut	4,580.

Grands

Model	Size	Style and Finish	Price*
152-C	5'	Polished Ebony	7,980.
152-C	5'	Polished Mahogany	8,380.
152-C	5'	Sapeli and Polished Sapeli Mahogany	8,380.
152-C	5'	Polished Cherry	8,380.
152-C	5'	Polished White	8,380.
152-DC	5'	Demi-Chippendale Polished Ebony	8,900.
152-DC	5'	Demi-Chippendale Polished Mahogany	9,180.
152-DC	5'	Demi-Chippendale Polished Walnut	9,180.
152-DC	5'	Demi-Chippendale Polished Sapeli	9,180.
165-CM	5' 5"	Polished Ebony	9,180.
165-CM	5' 5"	Polished Mahogany	9,500.
165-CM	5' 5"	Polished Walnut	9,500.
165-CM	5' 5"	Sapeli Mahogany	9,500.
165-DC	5' 5"	Demi-Chippendale Polished Ebony	10,180.
165-DC	5' 5"	Demi-Chippendale Polished Mahogany	10,500.
165-DC	5' 5"	Demi-Chippendale Polished Walnut	10,500.
165-PL	5' 5"	Walnut	9,900.
165-R	5' 5"	Regency Polished Ebony	9,780.
165-R	5' 5"	Regency Polished Mahogany	10,100.

Model	Size	Style and Finish	Price*
165-R	5' 5"	Regency Polished Walnut	10,100.
185-C	6' 1"	Polished Ebony	10,980.
185-C	6' 1"	Polished Mahogany	11,300.
185-C	6' 1"	Polished Walnut	11,300.
185-I	6' 1"	Imperial Polished Ebony	11,580.
185-I	6' 1"	Imperial Polished Mahogany	11,900.
185-I	6' 1"	Imperial Polished Walnut	11,900.
185-PN	6' 1"	Polished Ebony	11,380.
215	7'	Polished Ebony	19,980.
275	9'	Polished Ebony	51,800.

Palatino

Verticals
PUP-110	43-1/2"	Continental Polished Ebony	2,550.
PUP-110	43-1/2"	Continental Polished Walnut	2,550.
PUP-123	48-1/2"	Polished Ebony	2,940.
PUP-123	48-1/2"	Polished Walnut	2,940.
PUP-126	50"	Ebony and Polished Ebony	3,710.
PUP-126	50"	Polished Walnut	3,710.

Pearl River

Verticals
UP-108D3	42-1/2"	Continental Polished Ebony	2,640.
UP-108D3	42-1/2"	Continental Polished Mahogany	2,688.
UP-108D3	42-1/2"	Continental Polished Walnut	2,688.
UP-108D3	42-1/2"	Continental Polished White	2,742.
UP-108M2	42-1/2"	Demi-Chippendale Polished Ebony	2,884.
UP-108M2	42-1/2"	Demi-Chippendale Polished Mahogany	2,934.
UP-108M2	42-1/2"	Demi-Chippendale Polished Walnut	2,934.
UP-108T2	44"	Polished Ebony	3,212.
UP-108T2	44"	Polished Mahogany	3,264.
UP-108T2	44"	Polished Walnut	3,316.
UP-108T2	44"	Polished White	3,358.
UP-110P1	43-1/2"	Walnut	3,708.
UP-110P1	43-1/2"	Cherry	3,708.
UP-110P1	43-1/2"	Oak	3,762.
UP-110P2	43-1/2"	French Provincial Oak	3,986.

*For explanation of terms and prices, please see pages 54–60.

Model	Size	Style and Finish	Price*

Pearl River (continued)

Model	Size	Style and Finish	Price*
UP-110P2	43-1/2"	French Provincial Cherry	3,788.
UP-110P5	43"	Italian Provincial Walnut (Boston fall)	3,810.
UP-110P5	43"	Italian Provincial Cherry (Boston fall)	3,810.
UP-115M	45"	Polished Ebony	3,078.
UP-115M	45"	Polished Dark Mahogany	3,124.
UP-115M1	45"	Polished Ebony (school)	3,114.
UP-115M1	45"	Polished Dark Mahogany (school)	3,158.
UP-115M1	45"	Polished Walnut (school)	3,158.
UP-115P1	45"	Walnut	4,002.
UP-115P1	45"	Cherry	4,002.
UP-118E	46-1/2"	Polished Ebony	3,298.
UP-118E	46-1/2"	Polished Mahogany	3,348.
UP-118E	46-1/2"	Polished Walnut	3,348.
UP-118E	46-1/2"	Polished White	3,396.
UP-120S	48"	Polished Ebony	4,146.
UP-120S	48"	Polished Mahogany	4,248.
UP-125M1	49"	Polished Ebony (with Yamaha)	4,912.
UP-130T2	51-1/2"	Polished Mahogany w/Burl Oval Inlay	5,480.

Grands

Model	Size	Style and Finish	Price*
GP-142	4' 7"	Polished Ebony	7,872.
GP-142	4' 7"	Polished Mahogany	8,172.
GP-142	4' 7"	Polished Walnut	8,222.
GP-142	4' 7"	Polished White	8,314.
GP-142D	4' 7"	French Provincial Cherry	8,292.
GP-159	5' 3"	Ebony	10,464.
GP-159	5' 3"	Polished Ebony	10,164.
GP-159	5' 3"	Mahogany	10,588.
GP-159	5' 3"	Polished Mahogany	10,514.
GP-170	5' 7"	Ebony	13,614.
GP-170	5' 7"	Polished Ebony	13,314.
GP-170	5' 7"	Mahogany	13,708.
GP-170	5' 7"	Polished Mahogany	13,662.
GP-170D	5' 7"	French Provincial Cherry	13,720.
GP-183	6'	Polished Ebony	12,926.
GP-186	6' 1"	Polished Ebony	14,934.
GP-188	6' 4"	Polished Ebony	16,250.
GP-213	7'	Polished Ebony	19,550.
GP-275	9'	Polished Ebony	53,500.

Perzina, Gebr.

Verticals

Model	Size	Style and Finish	Price
GP-122BB	48"	Polished Ebony	6,890.
GP-122BC	48"	Polished Mahogany	7,190.
GP-122BC	48"	Polished Walnut	7,190.
GP-122C	48"	Ebony with Mahogany Center	7,190.
GP-122EB	48"	Queen Anne Polished Ebony	7,190.
GP-122EC	48"	Queen Anne Polished Mahogany	7,390.
GP-122EC	48"	Queen Anne Polished Walnut	7,390.
GP-126BB	49"	Polished Ebony	7,490.
GP-126BC	49"	Polished Mahogany	7,790.
GP-126BC	49"	Polished Walnut	7,790.
GP-126EB	49"	Queen Anne Polished Ebony	7,690.
GP-126EC	49"	Queen Anne Polished Mahogany	7,790.
GP-126EC	49"	Queen Anne Polished Walnut	7,790.
GP-129BB	51"	Polished Ebony	7,790.
GP-129BC	51"	Polished Mahogany	8,290.
GP-129BC	51"	Polished Walnut	8,290.
GP-129EB	51"	Queen Anne Polished Ebony	7,890.
GP-129EC	51"	Queen Anne Polished Mahogany	8,390.
GP-129EC	51"	Queen Anne Polished Walnut	8,390.

Grands

Model	Size	Style and Finish	Price
P-160BB	5' 3"	Polished Ebony	15,990.
P-160BC	5' 3"	Polished Mahogany	16,590.
P-160BC	5' 3"	Polished Walnut	16,590.
P-160BC	5' 3"	Polished Ivory	16,590.
P-160BC	5' 3"	Polished White	16,590.
P-160CB	5' 3"	Polished Ebony (round leg)	16,190.
P-160CC	5' 3"	Polished Mahogany (round leg)	16,790.
P-160CC	5' 3"	Polished Walnut (round leg)	16,790.
P-160EB	5' 3"	Queen Anne Polished Ebony	16,190.
P-160EC	5' 3"	Queen Anne Polished Mahogany	16,790.
P-160EC	5' 3"	Queen Anne Polished Walnut	16,790.
P-187BB	6' 1"	Polished Ebony	17,990.
P-187BC	6' 1"	Polished Mahogany	18,990.
P-187BC	6' 1"	Polished Walnut	18,990.
P-187BC	6' 1"	Polished Ivory	18,990.
P-187BC	6' 1"	Polished White	18,990.

*For explanation of terms and prices, please see pages 54–60.

Model	Size	Style and Finish	Price*

Petrof

Note: Prices below do not include bench. Add from $220 to $630 (most are under $400), depending on choice of bench.

Verticals

Model	Size	Style and Finish	Price*
115-I	46"	Chippendale Pol. Walnut w/Designer Panel	6,900.
115-I	46"	Chippendale Pol. Mahog. w/Designer Panel	6,900.
115-IC	46"	Chippendale Polished Walnut	6,980.
115-IC	46"	Chippendale Polished Mahogany	6,980.
115-II	46"	Polished Ebony	5,980.
115-II	46"	Polished Mahogany	5,980.
115-IID P/R	46"	Polished Ebony	6,780.
115-IID P/R	46"	Polished Walnut	6,780.
115-IID P/R	46"	Polished Mahogany	6,780.
115-V	46"	Polished Ebony	6,580.
115-V	46"	Polished Walnut	6,580.
115-V	46"	Polished Mahogany	6,580.
115-VI	46"	Polished Walnut	6,380.
115-VI	46"	Polished Walnut with Gold Marquetry	6,580.
115-VI	46"	Polished Walnut w/Designer Panel	6,500.
115-VI	46"	Polished Mahogany	6,380.
115-VI	46"	Polished Mahogany w/Designer Panel	6,500.
115-VI	46"	"Elegance" Pol. Ebony w/Walnut/Gold Trim	6,180.
115-VII	46"	Polished Burl Walnut Veneer	6,580.
125-III	49"	Polished Walnut	7,700.
125-III	49"	Polished Walnut with Fan Panels	7,900.
125-III	49"	Polished Mahogany	7,700.
125-III	49"	Polished Mahogany with Fan Panels	7,900.
125-IV	49"	Polished Ebony	7,780.
126	49"	"Elegante" Pol. Ebony w/Walnut/Gold Trim	8,300.
131	52"	Polished Ebony	10,500.
131	52"	Polished Walnut	10,500.
131	52"	Polished Mahogany	10,500.
135	53"	"Klasik" Polished Ebony	14,500.

Grands

Model	Size	Style and Finish	Price*
V	5' 3"	Polished Ebony	19,980.
V	5' 3"	Polished Walnut	19,980.
V	5' 3"	Polished Mahogany	19,980.
V DC	5' 3"	Demi-Chippendale Polished Ebony	22,400.
V DC	5' 3"	Demi-Chippendale Polished Walnut	22,400.

Model	Size	Style and Finish	Price*
V DC	5' 3"	Demi-Chippendale Polished Mahogany	22,400.
IV	5' 8"	Polished Ebony	21,600.
IV	5' 8"	Polished Walnut	21,600.
IV	5' 8"	Polished Mahogany	21,600.
IV C	5' 8"	Chippendale Polished Ebony	26,600.
IV C	5' 8"	Chippendale Polished Walnut	26,600.
IV C	5' 8"	Chippendale Polished Mahogany	26,600.
IV DC	5' 8"	Demi-Chippendale Polished Ebony	23,600.
IV DC	5' 8"	Demi-Chippendale Polished Walnut	23,600.
IV DC	5' 8"	Demi-Chippendale Polished Mahogany	23,600.
IV	5' 8"	"Klasik" Polished Ebony	25,600.
IV	5' 8"	"Klasik" Polished Walnut	25,600.
IV	5' 8"	"Klasik" Polished Mahogany	25,600.
III	6' 4"	Polished Ebony	25,800.
III	6' 4"	Polished Walnut	25,800.
III	6' 4"	Polished Mahogany	25,800.
III	6' 4"	"Majestic" Polished Ebony	27,800.
III	6' 4"	"Majestic" Polished Walnut	27,800.
III	6' 4"	"Majestic" Polished Mahogany	27,800.
II	7' 9"	Polished Ebony	39,000.
II	7' 9"	Polished Walnut	39,000.
I	9' 3"	"Mistral" Polished Ebony	62,000.

PianoDisc

Prices for PianoDisc and QuietTime systems vary by piano manufacturer and installer. The following are suggested retail prices from PianoDisc. The usual dealer discounts may apply, especially as an incentive to purchase a piano.

Opus7 "Opulence," "factory-installed" or retrofitted	18,357.
Opus7 "Luxury," "factory-installed" or retrofitted	14,276.
Opus7 Performance Package option	2,733.
228 CFX System, "factory-installed" or retrofitted:	
Playback only	6,635.
Add for SymphonyPro Sound Module	1,115.
Add for TFT MIDI Record system	1,627.
Add for amplified speakers, pair	735.
Add for MX (Music Expansion) Basic	1,171.
Add for MX (Music Expansion) Platinum	1,758.
Add for PianoMute Rail	664.
PianoCD System	5,995.

*For explanation of terms and prices, please see pages 54–60.

Model	Size	Style and Finish	Price*

PianoDisc (continued)

QuietTime GT System (TFT MIDI Strip, MIDI interface board,
         pedal switches, cable, headphones,
         power supply, PianoMute rail)   2,409.
MIDI Controller (TFT MIDI Strip, MIDI interface board,
         pedal switches, cable, power supply)   2,031.
AudioForte   2,447.

Pleyel

Verticals

Model	Size	Style and Finish	Price
Esprit	45"	Continental Polished Ebony	8,900.
Academie	45"	Polished Ebony	9,400.
Academie	45"	Walnut	9,800.
Academie	45"	Polished White	9,800.
P 118	47"	Polished Ebony	10,300.
P 118	47"	Polished Mahogany	12,100.
P 118	47"	*Walnut with Marquetry*	11,400.
P 118	47"	Cherry with Marquetry	11,400.
P 118	47"	"Romantica Noyer" Walnut	11,200.
P 124	49"	Polished Ebony	11,600.
P 124	49"	*Walnut with Marquetry*	13,000.
P 124	49"	Cherry with Marquetry	13,000.
P 131	51"	Polished Ebony	15,000.
P 131	51"	Polished Mahogany	15,900.
P 131	51"	*With Sostenuto, add*	700.

Grands

Model	Size	Style and Finish	Price
P 170	5' 7"	Polished Ebony	35,400.
P 170	5' 7"	Polished Mahogany	43,000.
P 170	5' 7"	Walnut	39,200.
P 190	6' 3"	Polished Ebony	43,000.
P 190	6' 3"	Cherry with Marquetry	50,700.
P 190	6' 3"	Polished Mahogany with Marquetry	50,700.

Pramberger

Verticals

Model	Size	Style and Finish	Price
JP-48	48"	Polished Ebony	7,390.
JP-48	48"	Brown Mahogany	7,990.

Model	Size	Style and Finish	Price*
JP-48	48"	Bubinga	7,990.
JP-48	48"	Rosewood	7,990.
JP-48	48"	Cherry	7,990.
JP-48	48"	Apple	8,790.
JP-52	52"	Polished Ebony	9,390.
JP-52	52"	Bubinga	9,990.
JP-52	52"	Rosewood	9,990.

Grands

Model	Size	Style and Finish	Price*
JP-175	5' 9"	Polished Ebony	18,590.
JP-175	5' 9"	Polished Ebony with Pommele Inlay	18,790.
JP-175	5' 9"	Polished Red Mahogany	19,790.
JP-175	5' 9"	Polished Brown Mahogany	19,790.
JP-175	5' 9"	Cherry	20,390.
JP-175	5' 9"	Polished Kewazinga Bubinga	20,590.
JP-185	6' 1"	Polished Ebony	21,990.
JP-185	6' 1"	Polished Ebony with Pommele Inlay	22,990.
JP-185	6' 1"	Polished Red Mahogany	23,990.
JP-185	6' 1"	Polished Brown Mahogany	23,990.
JP-185	6' 1"	Polished Kewazinga Bubinga	25,990.
JP-185	6' 1"	Polished Santos Rosewood	27,990.
JP-185	6' 1"	Cherry	28,990.
JP-185	6' 1"	Polished African Pommele	28,990.
JP-208	6' 10"	Polished Ebony	25,990.
JP-208	6' 10"	Polished Ebony with Pommele Inlay	27,190.
JP-208	6' 10"	Polished Kewazinga Bubinga	30,990.
JP-208	6' 10"	Polished Santos Rosewood	32,990.
JP-208	6' 10"	Polished Birch Burl	33,990.
JP-208	6' 10"	Polished African Pommele	34,500.
JP-228	7' 6"	Polished Ebony	36,390.
JP-228	7' 6"	*Polished Kewazinga Bubinga*	40,580.
JP-228	7' 6"	*Polished Santos Rosewood*	41,980.
JP-228	7' 6"	*Polished African Pommele*	42,780.

QRS / Pianomation

Prices for Pianomation systems vary by piano manufacturer, installer, and accessories. The following are approximate retail prices for installed systems from QRS. The usual dealer discounts may apply, especially as an incentive to purchase a piano.

Pianomation:	2000C Player System	5,220.

*For explanation of terms and prices, please see pages 54–60.

QRS / Pianomation (continued)

	2000CD+ Player System, CD player, speaker	5,975.
	Chili System with CD and	
	floppy drives, record strip, speaker	9,000.
	Serenade CD with CD drive, speaker	6,375.
	Serenade Pro with CD, floppy, and hard	
	drives, record strip, speaker	10,100.
Playola:	With 2000C Player System	6,000.
	With 2000CD+ Player System	6,750.
Practice Session with record strip, piano-only sound, stop rail		950.

Ritmüller

Verticals

Model	Size	Style and Finish	Price
UP-110R2	43-1/2"	"Elegant" Polished Ebony	3,246.
UP-110R2	43-1/2"	"Elegant" Polished Dark Mahogany	3,298.
UP-110R2	43-1/2"	"Elegant" Polished Walnut	3,298.
UP-118R2	46-1/2"	"Scandinavian Design" Polished Ebony	3,800.
UP-118R2	46-1/2"	"Scandinavian Design" Polished Mahogany	3,852.
UP-118R3	46-1/2"	Cherry	4,656.
UP-120R	48"	Polished Ebony	4,146.
UP-120R	48"	Polished Dark Mahogany	4,202.
UP-120R	48"	Polished Walnut	4,202.
UP-120R1	48"	"European Design" Pol. Ebony w/Mahog.	4,248.
UP-120R1	48"	"European Design" Teak w/Light Oak	4,300.
UP-120R2	48"	Chippendale Walnut	4,614.
UP-120R2	48"	Chippendale Mahogany	4,614.
UP-120R3	48"	"Euro-Modern" Polished Ebony	4,650.
UP-120R4	48"	French Provincial Cherry	4,614.
UP-123R	48"	"Classic Euro" Polished Ebony	5,136.
UP-123R	48"	"Classic Euro" Polished Mahogany	5,188.
UP-123R	48"	"Classic Euro" Polished Walnut	5,188.
UP-123R1	48"	"Deluxe European" Polished Ebony	5,150.
UP-125R	49"	"New-European" Pol. Ebony w/Mahogany	5,644.
UP-126R	50"	Polished Ebony (with Yamaha)	5,574.
UP-130R	51"	Polished Ebony (movable front)	5,692.
UP-130R	51"	Walnut (movable front)	5,746.
UP-130R	51"	Polished Dark Mahogany (movable front)	5,746.
UP-130R1	51"	Polished Ebony	5,658.

Model	Size	Style and Finish	Price*
Grands			
GP-142R	4' 7"	Ebony	8,480.
GP-142R	4' 7"	Polished Ebony	8,180.
GP-142R	4' 7"	Polished Mahogany	8,530.
GP-142R	4' 7"	Polished Walnut	8,530.
GP-142R1	4' 7"	Ebony (tapered leg, brass trim)	8,374.
GP-142R1	4' 7"	Polished Ebony (tapered leg, brass trim)	8,074.
GP-159R	5' 3"	Ebony	11,448.
GP-159R	5' 3"	Polished Ebony	11,148.
GP-159R	5' 3"	Mahogany	11,798.
GP-159R	5' 3"	Polished Mahogany	11,498.
GP-159R	5' 3"	Polished Walnut	11,498.
GP-159R1	5' 3"	Ebony (tapered leg, brass trim)	11,448.
GP-159R1	5' 3"	Polished Ebony (tapered leg, brass trim)	11,148.
GP-159R2	5' 3"	Louis XV Cherry	11,672.
GP-183R	6'	Ebony	14,650.
GP-183R	6'	Polished Ebony	14,350.
GP-183R1	6'	Ebony (tapered leg, brass trim)	14,544.
GP-183R1	6'	Polished Ebony (tapered leg, brass trim)	14,244.
GP-213R1	7'	Polished Ebony	20,122.
GP-275R1	9'	Polished Ebony	64,538.

Samick

Model	Size	Style and Finish	Price*
Verticals			
JS-042	42"	Continental Polished Ebony	2,750.
JS-042	42"	Continental Polished Mahogany	2,850.
JS-042	42"	Continental Polished Walnut	2,850.
JS-042	42"	Continental Cherry	2,850.
JS-042	42"	Continental Polished Ivory	2,850.
JS-143F	44"	French Provincial Cherry	3,590.
JS-143M	44"	Mediterranean Brown Oak	3,390.
JS-143T	44"	Mahogany	3,590.
JS-115	45"	Ebony	3,050.
JS-115	45"	Polished Ebony	2,950.
JS-115	45"	Satin/Polished Wood Finishes	3,050.
JS-115	45"	Polished Ivory	3,050.
JS-118F	46-1/2"	French Provincial Cherry	4,190.
JS-118M	46-1/2"	Mediterranean Brown Oak	3,990.
JS-118T	46-1/2"	Mahogany	4,190.

*For explanation of terms and prices, please see pages 54–60.

Model	Size	Style and Finish	Price*

Samick (continued)

Model	Size	Style and Finish	Price*
JS-247	46-1/2"	Ebony and Polished Ebony	4,700.
JS-247	46-1/2"	Satin and Polished Wood Finishes	4,700.
JS-121F	48"	French Provincial Polished Ebony	4,100.
JS-121F	48"	French Provincial Polished Mahogany	4,300.
JS-121M	48"	Mediterranean Polished Ebony	3,990.
JS-121M	48"	Mediterranean Polished Mahogany	4,270.

Grands

Model	Size	Style and Finish	Price*
SIG-50	4' 11-1/2"	Ebony	8,390.
SIG-50	4' 11-1/2"	Polished Ebony	8,190.
SIG-50	4' 11-1/2"	Polished Mahogany	8,790.
SIG-50	4' 11-1/2"	Polished Walnut	8,790.
SIG-50	4' 11-1/2"	Polished Ivory	8,790.
SIG-54	5' 3"	Ebony	9,390.
SIG-54	5' 3"	Polished Ebony	9,190.
SIG-54	5' 3"	Polished Mahogany	9,790.
SIG-54	5' 3"	Polished Walnut	9,790.
SIG-54	5' 3"	Polished Ivory	9,790.
SIG-54KBF	5' 3"	French Provincial Polished Mahogany	10,990.
SIG-54KBF	5' 3"	French Provincial Polished Cherry	10,990.
SIG-57	5' 7"	Ebony	10,190.
SIG-57	5' 7"	Polished Ebony	9,990.
SIG-57	5' 7"	Polished Mahogany	10,590.
SIG-57	5' 7"	Polished Walnut	10,590.
SIG-57	5' 7"	Polished Ivory	10,590.
SIG-57L	5' 7"	Empire Ebony	10,990.
SIG-57L	5' 7"	Empire Polished Ebony	10,790.
SIG-57L	5' 7"	Empire Polished Mahogany	11,590.
SIG-57L	5' 7"	Empire Polished Walnut	11,590.
SIG-57L	5' 7"	Empire Polished Ivory	11,590.
SIG-61	6' 1"	Ebony	10,990.
SIG-61	6' 1"	Polished Ebony	10,790.
SIG-61	6' 1"	Polished Mahogany	11,390.
SIG-61	6' 1"	Polished Walnut	11,390.
SIG-61	6' 1"	Polished Ivory	11,390.
SIG-61L	6' 1"	Empire Ebony	11,790.
SIG-61L	6' 1"	Empire Polished Ebony	11,590.
SIG-61L	6' 1"	Empire Polished Mahogany	12,190.
SIG-61L	6' 1"	Empire Polished Walnut	12,190.
SIG-61L	6' 1"	Empire Polished Ivory	12,190.

Model	Size	Style and Finish	Price*

Sängler & Söhne / Wieler

Verticals

Model	Size	Style and Finish	Price*
C43R	43"	Oak (round leg)	2,990.
C43R	43"	Mahogany (round leg)	2,900.
C43F	43"	French Oak	2,990.
C43F	43"	French Mahogany	2,990.
111GD	44"	Continental Polished Ebony	2,500.
111GD	44"	Continental Polished Mahogany	2,550.
111GD	44"	Continental Polished Walnut	2,550.
111GD	44"	Continental Polished White	2,550.
115GC	45"	Chippendale Polished Ebony	2,750.
115GC	45"	Chippendale Polished Mahogany	2,790.
450	45"	Italian Provincial Walnut	3,190.
450	45"	Italian Provincial Mahogany	3,190.
450	45"	Italian Provincial Cherry	3,190.
451	45"	Walnut (round leg)	3,190.
451	45"	Mahogany (round leg)	3,190.
451	45"	Cherry (round leg)	3,190.
452	45"	French Walnut	3,190.
452	45"	French Mahogany	3,190.
452	45"	French Cherry	3,190.
115WH	46"	Polished Ebony	2,790.
115WH	46"	Polished Mahogany	2,840.
115WH	46"	Polished Walnut	2,840.
121WH	48"	Polished Ebony	3,100.
121WH	48"	Polished Mahogany	3,100.
121WH	48"	Polished Walnut	3,100.
131X	52"	Polished Ebony	3,990.
131X	52"	Polished Mahogany	4,190.

*For explanation of terms and prices, please see pages 54–60.

Model	Size	Style and Finish	Price*

Sängler & Söhne / Wieler (continued)

Grands

Model	Size	Style and Finish	Price*
450	4' 7"	Polished Ebony	8,500.
450	4' 7"	Polished Mahogany	8,840.
450	4' 7"	Polished Brown Oak	8,840.
148SR	4' 11"	Victorian Polished Ebony	8,990.
148SR	4' 11"	Victorian Polished Mahogany	8,990.
148SR	4' 11"	Victorian Polished Walnut	8,990.
152DP	5'	Polished Ebony	7,990.
152DP	5'	Polished Mahogany	8,390.
152DP	5'	Polished Walnut	8,390.
152DP	5'	Polished White	8,390.
480	5' 1"	Polished Ebony	9,770.
480	5' 1"	Polished Mahogany	10,110.
165DP	5' 4"	Polished Ebony	8,590.
165DP	5' 4"	Polished Mahogany	9,190.
165DP	5' 4"	Polished Walnut	9,190.
165DP	5' 4"	Polished White	9,190.
185DP	6' 1"	Polished Ebony	9,990.
185DP	6' 1"	Polished Mahogany	10,390.

Sauter

Verticals

Model	Size	Style and Finish	Price*
122	48"	"Ragazza" Polished Ebony	20,040.
122	48"	"Ragazza" Cherry	19,730.
122	48"	"Ragazza" Polished Cherry/Yew	23,330.
122	48"	"Vista" Polished Ebony	21,830.
122	48"	"Vista" Maple	20,740.
122	48"	School Piano Open-pore Ebony	16,210.
122	48"	"M-Line M2" Polished Ebony	25,990.
122	48"	Peter Maly "Pure Noble" Polished Ebony	29,700.
128	51"	"M-Line M1" Polished Ebony	29,570.
128	51'"	"Competence" Polished Ebony	24,900.
128	51"	"Competence" Walnut	23,700.

Grands

Model	Size	Style and Finish	Price*
185	6' 1"	"Delta" Polished Ebony	55,050.
185	6' 1"	"Delta" Polished Pyramid Mahogany	61,130.
185	6' 1"	"Delta" Polished Bubinga	61,130.

Model	Size	Style and Finish	Price*
185	6' 1"	"Delta" Polished Rio Palisander	61,130.
185	6' 1"	"Delta" satin standard wood veneer	51,560.
206	6' 9"	Peter Maly "Vivace" Polished Ebony	81,350.
220	7' 3"	"Omega" Polished Ebony	70,290.
220	7' 3"	"Omega" Polished Pyramid Mahogany	77,830.
220	7' 3"	"Omega" satin standard wood veneer	66,280.
275	9'	"Concert" Polished Ebony	117,780.

Schell, Lothar

Verticals

LSU-110	43"	Polished Ebony	3,390.
LSU-110	43"	Polished Mahogany	3,590.
LSU-115F	45"	French Provincial Polished Ebony	3,590.
LSU-115F	45"	French Provincial Polished Mahogany	3,790.
LSU-45	45"	Mahogany and Polished Mahogany	3,790.
LSU-120	48"	Polished Ebony	3,900.
LSU-120	48"	Polished Mahogany	4,050.
LSU-122	48"	Polished Ebony	4,190.
LSU-122	48"	Polished Mahogany	4,340.

Grands

LG-152	5'	Polished Ebony	8,790.
LG-152	5'	Polished Mahogany	9,190.
LG-152F	5'	French Provincial Polished Ebony	9,390.
LG-152F	5'	French Provincial Polished Mahogany	9,690.
LG-152R	5'	Polished Ebony (round legs)	9,390.
LG-152R	5'	Polished Mahogany (round legs)	9,790.
LG-165	5' 5"	Polished Ebony	9,590.
LG-165	5' 5"	Polished Mahogany	9,990.
LG-165F	5' 5"	French Provincial Polished Ebony	10,190.
LG-165F	5' 5"	French Provincial Polished Mahogany	10,590.
LG-165R	5' 5"	Polished Ebony (round legs)	10,190.
LG-165R	5' 5"	Polished Mahogany (round legs)	10,590.
LG-185	6' 1"	Polished Ebony	11,590.
LG-185	6' 1"	Polished Mahogany	11,990.
LG-185F	6' 1"	French Provincial Polished Ebony	12,190.
LG-185F	6' 1"	French Provincial Polished Mahogany	12,590.
LG-185R	6' 1"	Polished Ebony (round legs)	12,190.
LG-185R	6' 1"	Polished Mahogany (round legs)	12,590.
LG-215	7' 1"	Polished Ebony	18,290.

*For explanation of terms and prices, please see pages 54–60.

Model	Size	Style and Finish	Price*

Schimmel

Verticals

Model	Size	Style and Finish	Price*
112 S	44"	Open-Pore Ebony	14,180.
112 S	44"	Open-Pore Oak	14,180.
112 S	44"	Open-Pore Walnut	14,180.
116 AD	46"	"Art Deco" Polished Ebony	13,980.
116 E	46"	"Exquisite" Polished Ebony	14,180.
116 E	46"	"Exquisite" Polished Mahogany	14,780.
116 E	46"	"Exquisite" Polished White	14,780.
116 E	46"	"Exquisite" Open-Pore Waxed Alder	14,580.
116 E	46"	"Exquisite" Open-Pore Walnut	14,580.
116 E	46"	"Exquisite" Open-Pore Walnut w/Intarsia	15,380.
116 E	46"	"Exquisite" Open-Pore Beech	14,580.
116 E	46"	"Exquisite" Waxed Plum	14,580.
116 E	46"	"Exquisite" O.P. Waxed Swiss Pear	14,580.
116 ST	46"	Polished Ebony	12,980.
120 I	48"	"International" Polished Ebony	14,580.
120 I	48"	"International" Polished Mahogany	15,180.
120 I	48"	"International" Pol. Mahogany w/Intarsia	15,580.
120 I	48"	"International" Polished White	15,180.
120 J	48"	"Centennial" Pol. Mahog. with Myrtle Inlay	15,380.
120 J	48"	"Centennial" Pol. Cherry with Yew Inlay	15,780.
120 RI	48"	"Royale Intarsia" Polished Mahogany	16,980.
120 RI	48"	"Royale Intarsia" Cherry	16,980.
120 S	48"	"School" Open-Pore Ebony	14,780.
120 S	48"	"School" Open-Pore Oak	14,780.
120 TR	48"	Polished Ebony	14,980.
120 TR	48"	Waxed Swiss Pear	15,380.
122 KE	49"	"Classic Exquisite" Polished Ebony	15,180.
122 KE	49"	"Classic Exquisite" Polished Mahogany	15,780.
122 KE	49"	"Classic Exquisite" O.P. Waxed Alder	15,980.
122 KE	49"	"Classic Exquisite" Cherry	15,980.
F 122 AC	49"	"Art Cubus" Polished Ebony	16,980.
F 122 AC	49"	"Art Cubus" Waxed Swiss Pear	17,380.
F 122 SE	49"	"Salon Exquisite" Polished Ebony	16,180.
124 TC	49"	Polished Ebony	15,980.
124 TC	49"	Polished Ebony w/Oval Decoration	16,580.
124 TC	49"	Polished Mahogany	16,580.
124 TC	49"	Polished Mahogany w/Oval Decoration	17,180.
S 125 DN	49"	"Diamond Noblesse" Polished Ebony	18,780.

Model	Size	Style and Finish	Price*
S 125 DN	49"	"Diamond Noblesse" Polished Mahogany	19,580.
S 125 DP	49"	"Diamond Prestige" Polished Ebony	19,180.
S 125 DP	49"	"Diamond Prestige" Polished Mahogany	19,980.
130 T	51"	Polished Ebony	17,180.
130 T	51"	Polished Ebony w/Oval Decoration	17,780.
130 T	51"	Polished Mahogany	17,780.
130 T	51"	Open-Pore Walnut	18,580.
130 T	51"	Polished Walnut	17,780.
O 132 DT	52"	"Diamond Tradition" Polished Ebony	19,980.
O 132 DT	52"	"Diamond Tradition" Pol. Mahogany	20,980.
O 132 EM	52"	"Edition Manufactum" Mahogany	34,980.
O 132 EM	52"	"Edition Manufactum" Walnut	34,980.

Grands

When not mentioned, satin finish available on special order at same price as high-polish finish.

Model	Size	Style and Finish	Price*
GP 169 DE	5' 7"	"Diamond Edition" Polished Ebony	40,180.
GP 169 DE	5' 7"	"Diamond Edition" Pol. Flame Mahogany	43,780.
GP 169 DE	5' 7"	"Diamond Edition" Polished Bubinga	43,780.
GP 169 DE	5' 7"	"Diamond Edition" Pol. Bird's-Eye Maple	43,780.
GP 169 DE	5' 7"	"Diamond Edition" Macassar	43,780.
GP 169 DE	5' 7"	"Diamond Edition" Polished White	43,780.
GP 169 E	5' 7"	"Empire" Mahogany and Pol. Mahogany	48,180.
GP 169 T	5' 7"	Polished Ebony	37,180.
GP 169 T	5' 7"	Polished Mahogany	38,380.
GP 169 T	5' 7"	Polished White	38,380.
GP 169 T	5' 7"	"Hidden Beauty" Pol. Ebony w/Bubinga	39,980.
GP 169 TE	5' 7"	"Exquisite" Polished Ebony	39,980.
GP 169 TE	5' 7"	"Exquisite" Polished Mahogany	41,180.
GP 169 TE	5' 7"	"Exquisite" Polished White	41,180.
GP 169 TE-I	5' 7"	"Exquisite" Polished Mahogany Intarsia	41,780.
GP 169 TJ	5' 7"	"Centennial" Polished Ebony	39,580.
GP 169 TJ	5' 7"	"Centennial" Polished Mahogany	40,780.
GP 169 TJ	5' 7"	"Centennial" Polished White	40,780.
SP 189 DE	6' 3"	"Diamond Edition" Polished Ebony	44,380.
SP 189 DE	6' 3"	"Diamond Edition" Pol. Flame Mahogany	47,980.
SP 189 DE	6' 3"	"Diamond Edition" Polished Bubinga	47,980.
SP 189 DE	6' 3"	"Diamond Edition" Pol. Bird's-Eye Maple	47,980.
SP 189 DE	6' 3"	"Diamond Edition" Macassar	47,980.
SP 189 DE	6' 3"	"Diamond Edition" Polished White	47,980.

*For explanation of terms and prices, please see pages 54–60.

Model	Size	Style and Finish	Price*

Schimmel (continued)

Model	Size	Style and Finish	Price*
SP 189 E	6' 3"	"Empire" Mahogany and Pol. Mahogany	52,180.
SP 189 NWS	6' 3"	"Nikolaus W. Schimmel Special Edition"	53,780.
SP 189 T	6' 3"	Polished Ebony	41,380.
SP 189 T	6' 3"	Polished Walnut	42,580.
SP 189 T	6' 3"	Polished Mahogany	42,580.
SP 189 T	6' 3"	Polished White	42,580.
SP 189 T	6' 3"	"Hidden Beauty" Pol. Ebony w/Bubinga	44,380.
SP 189 TE	6' 3"	"Exquisite" Polished Ebony	44,180.
SP 189 TE	6' 3"	"Exquisite" Polished Mahogany	45,380.
SP 189 TE	6' 3"	"Exquisite" Polished White	45,380.
SP 189 TE-I	6' 3"	"Exquisite" Polished Mahogany Intarsia	45,980.
SP 189 TJ	6' 3"	"Centennial" Polished Ebony	43,980.
SP 189 TJ	6' 3"	"Centennial" Polished Mahogany	44,980.
SP 189 TJ	6' 3"	"Centennial" Polished Cherry	44,980.
CC 213 ART	7'	"Art Edition" Pol. Ebony w/color motifs	141,000.
CC 213 DE	7'	"Diamond Edition" Polished Ebony	48,580.
CC 213 DE	7'	"Diamond Edition" Pol. Flame Mahogany	52,180.
CC 213 DE	7'	"Diamond Edition" Polished Bubinga	52,180.
CC 213 DE	7'	"Diamond Edition" Pol. Bird's-Eye Maple	52,180.
CC 213 DE	7'	"Diamond Edition" Macassar	52,180.
CC 213 DE	7'	"Diamond Edition" Polished White	52,180.
CC 213 G	7'	*Plexiglass Clear Acrylic and White*	119,000.
CC 213 NWS	7'	"Nikolaus W. Schimmel Special Edition"	57,980.
CC 213 T	7'	Polished Ebony	45,580.
CC 213 T	7'	Polished Mahogany	46,780.
CC 213 T	7'	Polished Walnut	46,780.
CC 213 T	7'	Polished White	46,780.
CC 213 T	7'	"Hidden Beauty" Pol. Ebony w/Bubinga	48,580.
CC 213 TE	7'	"Exquisite" Polished Ebony	48,380.
CC 213 TE	7'	"Exquisite" Polished Mahogany	49,580.
CC 213 TE	7'	"Exquisite" Polished White	49,580.
CC 213 TJ	7'	"Centennial" Polished Ebony	47,980.
CC 213 TJ	7'	"Centennial" Polished Mahogany	49,180.
CC 213 TJ	7'	"Centennial" Polished White	49,180.
CO 256 T	8' 4"	Polished Ebony	73,000.

Model	Size	Style and Finish	Price*

Schultz & Sons

Model numbers beginning with 3 or 4 designate pianos manufactured by Broadwood, numbers beginning with 7 or 8, by Samick.

Verticals

Model	Size	Style and Finish	Price*
3807-S	47"	Walnut	18,550.
3807-S	47"	Polished Walnut	20,750.
3807-S	47"	Mahogany	18,550.
3807-S	47"	Polished Mahogany	20,750.
3809-S	47"	Polished Mahogany	25,550.
3819-S	47"	Walnut	20,995.
3819-S	47"	Polished Walnut	22,995.
3819-S	47"	Mahogany	20,995.
3819-S	47"	Polished Mahogany	22,995.
7703-S	47-1/2"	Polished Mahogany	10,750.
7703-S	47-1/2"	Polished Cherry	10,750.
7703-SCC	47-1/2"	*Custom Finish*	13,850.
7708-S	47-1/2"	Polished Mahogany	10,750.
7708-S	47-1/2"	Polished Cherry	10,750.
7708-SCC	47-1/2"	*Custom Finish*	13,850.
7707-U	48-1/2"	Ebony and Polished Ebony	11,595.
7707-U	48-1/2"	Walnut and Polished Walnut	12,550.
7707-U	48-1/2"	Polished Mahogany	12,550.
3817-U	50"	Polished Ebony	25,750.
3817-U	50"	Walnut	23,995.
3817-U	50"	Polished Walnut	26,850.
3817-U	50"	Mahogany	23,995.
3817-U	50"	Polished Mahogany	26,850.
7717-U	52"	Ebony and Polished Ebony	12,550.
7717-U	52"	Walnut and Polished Walnut	13,250.
7717-U	52"	Polished Mahogany	13,250.

Grands

Model	Size	Style and Finish	Price*
8501-B	5' 2"	Ebony and Polished Ebony	18,450.
8501-B	5' 2"	Walnut and Polished Walnut	19,350.
8501-B	5' 2"	Polished Mahogany	19,350.
8501-B	5' 2"	Polished Ivory/White	18,750.
8601-B	5' 2"	Ebony and Polished Ebony	25,995.
8601-B	5' 2"	Walnut and Polished Walnut	26,950.
8601-B	5' 2"	Polished Mahogany	26,950.
8601-B	5' 2"	Polished Ivory/White	26,250.

*For explanation of terms and prices, please see pages 54–60.

Model	Size	Style and Finish	Price*

Schultz & Sons (continued)

Model	Size	Style and Finish	Price*
10501-B	5' 5"	Ebony and Polished Ebony	19,595.
10501-B	5' 5"	Walnut and Polished Walnut	20,350.
10501-B	5' 5"	Polished Mahogany	20,350.
10501-B	5' 5"	Polished Ivory/White	19,998.
8601-M	5' 9-1/2"	"Classic" Ebony and Polished Ebony	20,595.
8601-M	5' 9-1/2"	"Classic" Walnut and Polished Walnut	21,695.
8601-M	5' 9-1/2"	"Classic" Polished Mahogany	21,695.
8601-M	5' 9-1/2"	"Classic" Polished Ivory/White	21,150.
8701-M	5' 9-1/2"	"Classic" Ebony and Polished Ebony	27,495.
8701-M	5' 9-1/2"	"Classic" Walnut and Polished Walnut	28,395.
8701-M	5' 9-1/2"	"Classic" Polished Mahogany	28,395.
8701-M	5' 9-1/2"	"Classic" Polished Ivory/White	27,995.
8721-M	5' 9-1/2"	"Victorian" Ebony and Polished Ebony	22,995.
8721-M	5' 9-1/2"	"Victorian" Walnut and Polished Walnut	23,750.
8721-M	5' 9-1/2"	"Victorian" Polished Mahogany	23,750.
8721-M	5' 9-1/2"	"Victorian" Polished Ivory/White	23,550.
8821-M	5' 9-1/2"	"Victorian" Ebony and Polished Ebony	29,750.
8821-M	5' 9-1/2"	"Victorian" Walnut and Polished Walnut	30,695.
8821-M	5' 9-1/2"	"Victorian" Polished Mahogany	30,695.
8821-M	5' 9-1/2"	"Victorian" Polished Ivory/White	30,450.
8741-M	5' 9-1/2"	Polished Mahogany with Floral Inlays	28,995.
8741-MCC	5' 9-1/2"	*Custom Finish with Floral Inlays*	35,750.
8741-MCS	5' 9-1/2"	*Custom Finish with Custom Inlays*	on request
8731-M	5' 9-1/2"	Louis XV Ebony and Polished Ebony	25,995.
8731-M	5' 9-1/2"	Louis XV Walnut and Polished Walnut	26,895.
8731-M	5' 9-1/2"	Louis XV Polished Mahogany	26,895.
8731-M	5' 9-1/2"	Louis XV Polished Ivory/White	26,550.
4908-L	6'	"Euro Classic" Ebony	65,550.
4908-L	6'	"Euro Classic" Polished Ebony	68,095.
10601-L	6' 1"	"Classic" Ebony and Polished Ebony	22,249.
8701-L	6' 1"	"Classic" Ebony and Polished Ebony	22,250.
8701-L	6' 1"	"Classic" Walnut and Polished Walnut	23,095.
8701-L	6' 1"	"Classic" Polished Mahogany	23,095.
8701-L	6' 1"	"Classic" Polished Ivory/White	22,550.
8801-L	6' 1"	"Classic" Ebony and Polished Ebony	29,195.
8801-L	6' 1"	"Classic" Walnut and Polished Walnut	29,950.
8801-L	6' 1"	"Classic" Polished Mahogany	29,950.
8801-L	6' 1"	"Classic" Polished Ivory/White	29,250.
8709-L	6' 1"	"Victorian" Ebony and Polished Ebony	24,450.

Model	Size	Style and Finish	Price*
8709-L	6' 1"	"Victorian" Walnut and Polished Walnut	25,550.
8709-L	6' 1"	"Victorian" Polished Mahogany	25,550.
8709-L	6' 1"	"Victorian" Polished Ivory/White	24,750.
8809-L	6' 1"	"Victorian" Ebony and Polished Ebony	31,995.
8809-L	6' 1"	"Victorian" Walnut and Polished Walnut	33,050.
8809-L	6' 1"	"Victorian" Polished Mahogany	33,050.
8809-L	6' 1"	"Victorian" Polished Ivory/White	32,950.
8811-X	6' 9"	Ebony and Polished Ebony	38,995.
8811-SX	7' 1"	Ebony and Polished Ebony	43,895.

Schulze Pollmann

Verticals

114	45"	Polished Ebony	6,790.
114	45"	Polished Mahogany	6,990.
114	45"	Polished Peacock Mahogany	7,190.
114	45"	Polished Walnut	6,990.
114	45"	Polished Peacock Walnut	7,190.
114/R	45"	Polished Ebony	7,590.
114/R	45"	Polished Mahogany	7,790.
114/R	45"	Polished Peacock Mahogany	8,390.
114/R	45"	Polished Walnut	7,790.
114/R	45"	Polished Peacock Walnut	8,390.
118/P8	46"	Polished Ebony	11,590.
118/P8	46"	Polished Walnut	12,590.
118/P8	46"	Polished Mahogany	12,590.
126	50"	Polished Ebony	13,990.
126	50"	Oval Mahogany	14,590.
126	50"	Polished Mahogany	14,590.
126	50"	Walnut and Polished Walnut	14,590.
126	50"	Polished Cherry	14,590.

Grands

160	5' 3"	Polished Ebony	28,790.
160	5' 3"	Polished Walnut	31,390.
160	5' 3"	Polished Briar Walnut	33,190.
160	5' 3"	Polished Mahogany	32,990.
160	5' 3"	Polished Briar Mahogany	33,190.
160	5' 3"	Polished Ebony (round leg)	29,790.
160	5' 3"	Polished Walnut (round leg)	32,390.
160	5' 3"	Chippendale Polished Walnut	34,390.

*For explanation of terms and prices, please see pages 54–60.

Model	Size	Style and Finish	Price*

Schulze Pollmann (continued)

Model	Size	Style and Finish	Price*
160	5' 3"	Chippendale Polished Mahogany	34,390.
160/R	5' 3"	Polished Ebony	32,790.
160/R	5' 3"	Polished Mahogany	34,790.
160/R	5' 3"	Polished Briar Mahogany	35,190.
160/R	5' 3"	Polished Walnut	34,790.
160/R	5' 3"	Polished Briar Walnut	35,190.
160/R	5' 3"	Polished Peacock Walnut	37,390.
190F	6' 3"	Polished Ebony	41,590.
190F	6' 3"	Polished Mahogany	44,990.
190F	6' 3"	Polished Briar Mahogany	45,390.
190F	6' 3"	Polished Walnut	44,990.
190F	6' 3"	Polished Briar Walnut	45,390.
197A	6' 7"	Polished Ebony	46,990.
197A	6' 7"	Polished Briar Mahogany	51,990.
197A	6' 7"	Polished Briar Walnut	51,990.

Seidl & Sohn

Prices do not include bench.

Verticals

Model	Size	Style and Finish	Price*
SL 109	43"	Continental Polished Ebony	6,726.
SL 109	43"	Continental Polished Walnut	6,726.
SL 109	43"	Continental Polished Flame Mahogany	6,726.
SL 109	43"	Continental Polished White	6,873.
SL 113	46"	Polished Ebony	6,894.
SL 113	46"	Polished Walnut	6,894.
SL 113	46"	Polished Flame Mahogany	6,894.
SL 113	46"	Polished White	7,041.
SL 117	47"	Chippendale Polished Walnut	7,459.
SL 117	47"	Chippendale Polished Mahogany	7,459.
SL 120	48"	Polished Ebony	7,250.
SL 120	48"	Polished Walnut	7,250.
SL 120	48"	Polished Flame Mahogany	7,250.
SL 120	48"	Polished White	7,417.
SL 127	51"	Polished Ebony	8,276.
SL 127	51"	Polished Walnut	8,276.
SL 127	51"	Polished Mahogany	8,276.
SL 120/127		*Renner Action, add'l*	639.

Model	Size	Style and Finish	Price*

Seiler

Verticals

Model	Size	Style and Finish	Price*
116	46"	"Mondial" Open-Pore Ebony	15,060.
116	46"	"Mondial" Open-Pore Walnut	15,060.
116	46"	"Mondial" Open-Pore Mahogany	15,060.
116	46"	"Mondial" Polished Mahogany	15,760.
116	46"	"Mondial" Open-Pore Oak	15,060.
116	46"	"Mondial" Open-Pore Maple	15,220.
116	46"	"Mondial" Open-Pore Cherry	16,040.
116	46"	"Mondial" Alderwood	15,220.
116	46"	"Mondial" Open-Pore Swiss Pear	15,540.
116	46"	"Mondial" Open-Pore Apple Heartwood	16,040.
116	46"	"Mondial" Polished Burl Rosewood	17,420.
116	46"	"Jubilee" Polished Ebony	16,160.
116	46"	"Jubilee" Polished White	16,420.
116	46"	Chippendale Open-Pore Walnut	15,220.
116	46"	"Escorial" Open-Pore Cherry, Intarsia	16,420.
122	48"	"Konsole" Open-Pore Ebony	15,680.
122	48"	"Konsole" Polished Ebony	16,740.
122	48"	"Konsole" Open-Pore Walnut	15,680.
122	48"	"Konsole" Polished Walnut Rootwood	22,660.
122	48"	"Konsole" Open-Pore Oak	15,680.
122	48"	"Konsole" Open-Pore Maple	15,680.
122	48"	"Konsole" Maple Burl	16,300.
122	48"	"Konsole" Open-Pore Cherry	16,440.
122	48"	"Konsole" Polished Burl Rosewood	19,360.
122	48"	"Konsole" Polished Brown Ash	19,360.
122	48"	"Konsole" Polished Redwood Burl	20,340.
122	48"	"Konsole" Polished White	17,300.
122	48"	"School" Open-Pore Ebony	14,960.
122	48"	"School" Open-Pore Walnut	14,960.
122	48"	"School" Open-Pore Oak	14,960.
122	48"	"Vienna" Polished Ebony w/Pilaster	17,200.
122	48"	"Vienna" Polished Ebony w/Pilaster & Oval	17,360.
122	48"	"Vienna" Pol. Mahogany w/ Flower Inlays	19,360.
122	48"	"Vienna" Polished Walnut w/ Flower Inlays	19,360.
122	48"	"Vienna" Maple with Pilaster	17,200.
122	48"	"Vienna" Maple with Pilaster & Oval	17,360.

*For explanation of terms and prices, please see pages 54–60.

Model	Size	Style and Finish	Price*

Seiler (continued)

Model	Size	Style and Finish	Price*
132	52"	"Concert SMR" Polished Ebony	21,320.
132	52"	"Concert SMR" Polished Ebony w/Oval	21,960.
132	52"	"Concert SMR" Polished Ebony w/Candle	21,920.
132	52"	"Concert SMR" Polished Ebony w/Panels	22,060.
132	52"	"Concert SMR" Open-Pore Walnut	20,680.
132	52"	"Concert SMR" Polished Mahogany	21,980.
132	52"	"Concert SMR" Polished Burl Rosewood	23,480.
132	52"	"Concert SMR" Polished Yew	25,280.
132	52"	"Concert SMR" Polished Ash Rootwood	25,280.
132	52"	"Concert SMR" Polished Burl Maple	26,140.
132	52"	"Limited Edition" Polished Ebony	24,580.
132	52"	"Limited Ed." Pol. Ebony w/Oval or Pilaster	25,080.
132	52"	"Limited Ed." Pol. Ebony w/Oval & Pilaster	25,580.

Grands

Model	Size	Style and Finish	Price*
186	6' 1"	"Maestro" Polished Ebony	47,180.
186	6' 1"	"Maestro" Open-Pore Walnut	47,180.
186	6' 1"	"Maestro" Polished Walnut	50,320.
186	6' 1"	"Maestro" Open-Pore Mahogany	47,180.
186	6' 1"	"Maestro" Polished Mahogany	50,320.
186	6' 1"	"Maestro" Polished Pyramid Mahogany	66,060.
186	6' 1"	"Maestro" Polished Burl Rosewood	58,880.
186	6' 1"	"Maestro" Polished Flamed Maple	59,480.
186	6' 1"	"Maestro" Polished Peacock Maple	66,060.
186	6' 1"	"Maestro" Polished White	48,220.
186	6' 1"	Chippendale Open-Pore Walnut	50,200.
186	6' 1"	"Westminster" Polished Mahogany, Intarsia	66,060.
186	6' 1"	"Florenz" Polished Walnut/Myrtle, Intarsia	66,060.
186	6' 1"	"Florenz" Polished Mahog./Myrtle, Intarsia	66,060.
186	6' 1"	"Louvre" Polished Ebony	52,960.
186	6' 1"	"Louvre" Polished Cherry, Intarsia	66,060.
186	6' 1"	"Louvre" Polished White	53,880.
186	6' 1"	"Prado" Polished Brown Ash	67,940.
186	6' 1"	"Prado" Polished Burl Redwood	70,360.
186	6' 1"	"Stella" Polished Maple Rootwood, Intarsia	81,140.
186	6' 1"	"Meridian" Pol. Maple Rootwood Intarsia	81,140.
186	6' 1"	"Concordia" Pol. Peacock Maple Intarsia	81,140.
186	6' 1"	"Showmaster" Chrome/Brass/Polyester	131,580.
208	6' 10"	Polished Ebony	54,220.
208	6' 10"	"Empire 1897" Open-Pore Blue w/Brass	167,700.

Model	Size	Style and Finish	Price*
208	6' 10"	"Solitaire" Custom with Painting	189,020.
208	6' 10"	"Solitaire" Custom without Painting	153,460.
242	8'	Polished Ebony	73,700.
278	9' 1"	Polished Ebony	

Sejung

See also under "Cable, Hobart M.,," "Falcone," and "Steck, Geo."

Verticals

U 09	43"	Continental Polished Ebony	2,870.
U 09	43"	Continental Polished Mahogany	2,990.
U 09	43"	Continental Polished Walnut	2,990.
U 09	43"	Continental Polished White	2,990.
C 12F	44"	French Provincial Cherry	3,370.
C 12F	44"	French Provincial Oak	3,370.
C 12M	44"	Mediterranean Cherry	3,370.
C 12M	44"	Mediterranean Oak	3,370.
U 12T	44"	Polished Ebony	3,080.
U 12T	44"	Polished Mahogany	3,200.
U 12T	44"	Polished Walnut	3,200.
U 19T	47"	Polished Ebony	3,200.
U 19T	47"	Polished Mahogany	3,320.
U 19T	47"	Polished Walnut	3,320.
U 32T	52"	Polished Ebony	3,620.

Grands

G 42	4' 8"	Polished Ebony	8,420.
G 42	4' 8"	Polished Mahogany	8,820.
G 42	4' 8"	Polished Walnut	8,820.
G 42	4' 8"	Polished White	8,620.
G 62	5' 4"	Polished Ebony	10,290.
G 62	5' 4"	Polished Mahogany	10,690.
G 62	5' 4"	Polished Walnut	10,690.
G 62	5' 4"	Polished White	10,490.
G 72	5' 8"	Polished Ebony	11,320.
G 72	5' 8"	Polished Mahogany	11,720.
G 72	5' 8"	Polished Walnut	11,720.

*For explanation of terms and prices, please see pages 54–60.

Sohmer (Persis International)

Verticals

Model	Size	Style and Finish	Price
S-50	50"	Polished Ebony	6,990.
S-50	50"	Polished Mahogany	7,190.

Grands

Model	Size	Style and Finish	Price
A	5' 3"	Polished Ebony	16,390.
A	5' 3"	Polished Mahogany	16,790.
B	5' 10"	Polished Ebony	18,790.
B	5' 10"	Polished Mahogany	19,190.
C	7' 2"	Polished Ebony	31,990.

Sohmer & Co. (SMC)

Verticals

Model	Size	Style and Finish	Price
34F	42"	French Provincial Semi-Gloss Cherry	5,590.
34R	42"	Renaissance Semi-Gloss Walnut	5,590.
34R	42"	Renaissance Semi-Gloss Cherry	5,590.
34T	42"	Semi-Gloss Mahogany	5,590.
34T	42"	Semi-Gloss Walnut	5,590.

Grands

Model	Size	Style and Finish	Price
50F	5'	French Provincial Semi-Gloss Mahogany	17,190.
50F	5'	French Provincial Semi-Gloss Cherry	17,190.
50T	5'	Ebony	13,990.
50T	5'	Semi-Gloss Mahogany	15,190.
50T	5'	Semi-Gloss Walnut	15,190.
50T	5'	Semi-Gloss Cherry	15,190.
63E	5' 4"	Empire Semi-Gloss Mahogany	16,990.
63E	5' 4"	Empire Semi-Gloss Walnut	16,990.
63E	5' 4"	Empire Semi-Gloss Cherry	16,990.
63F	5' 4"	French Provincial Semi-Gloss Mahogany	17,790.
63F	5' 4"	French Provincial Semi-Gloss Walnut	17,790.
63F	5' 4"	French Provincial Semi-Gloss Cherry	17,790.
63H	5' 4"	Hepplewhite Semi-Gloss Mahogany	17,190.
63H	5' 4"	Hepplewhite Semi-Gloss Walnut	17,190.
63H	5' 4"	Hepplewhite Semi-Gloss Cherry	17,190.
63T	5' 4"	Ebony	14,590.
63T	5' 4"	Semi-Gloss Mahogany	15,790.
63T	5' 4"	Semi-Gloss Walnut	15,790.
63T	5' 4"	Semi-Gloss Cherry	15,790.

Model	Size	Style and Finish	Price*
77E	5' 9"	Empire Semi-Gloss Mahogany	17,390.
77E	5' 9"	Empire Semi-Gloss Walnut	17,390.
77E	5' 9"	Empire Semi-Gloss Cherry	17,390.
77F	5' 9"	French Provincial Semi-Gloss Mahogany	18,190.
77F	5' 9"	French Provincial Semi-Gloss Walnut	18,190.
77F	5' 9"	French Provincial Semi-Gloss Cherry	18,190.
77H	5' 9"	Hepplewhite Semi-Gloss Mahogany	17,190.
77H	5' 9"	Hepplewhite Semi-Gloss Walnut	17,190.
77H	5' 9"	Hepplewhite Semi-Gloss Cherry	17,190.
77T	5' 9"	Ebony	14,990.
77T	5' 9"	Semi-Gloss Mahogany	16,190.
77T	5' 9"	Semi-Gloss Walnut	16,190.
77T	5' 9"	Semi-Gloss Cherry	16,190.
90H	6' 2"	Hepplewhite Semi-Gloss Mahogany	17,390.
90H	6' 2"	Hepplewhite Semi-Gloss Walnut	17,390.
90H	6' 2"	Hepplewhite Semi-Gloss Cherry	17,390.
90T	6' 2"	Ebony	15,190.
90T	6' 2"	Semi-Gloss Mahogany	16,390.
95T	6' 8"	Ebony	21,200.
95T	6' 8"	Semi-Gloss Mahogany	22,200.
95T	6' 8"	Semi-Gloss Walnut	22,200.
95T	6' 8"	Semi-Gloss Cherry	22,200.

Steck, Geo.

Available finishes include: Ebony, Polished Ebony, Brown Mahogany, Polished Mahogany, Walnut, Polished Walnut, Brown Oak, Polished Red Oak, Cherry, Polished White, Polished Ivory.

Verticals

Model	Size	Style and Finish	Price*
US 09L	43"	Continental Polished Ebony	2,950.
US 09L	43"	Continental Brown Oak	2,990.
US 09L	43"	Continental Walnut	2,990.
US 09L	43"	Continental Cherry	2,990.
US 09L	43"	Continental Other Finishes	3,070.
CS 12F	44"	French Provincial Brown Oak	3,370.
CS 12F	44"	French Provincial Cherry	3,370.
CS 12M	44"	Mediterranean Brown Oak	3,370.
CS 12M	44"	Mediterranean Cherry	3,370.
US 12T	44"	Polished Ebony	3,080.

*For explanation of terms and prices, please see pages 54–60.

Model	Size	Style and Finish	Price*

Steck, Geo. (continued)

Model	Size	Style and Finish	Price*
US 12T	44"	Brown Oak	3,120.
US 12T	44"	Walnut	3,120.
US 12T	44"	Cherry	3,120.
US 12T	44"	Other Finishes	3,200.
CS 16AT	45"	Brown Oak	3,650.
CS 16AT	45"	Cherry	3,650.
CS 16AT	45"	Mahogany	3,650.
CS 16F	45"	French Provincial Cherry	3,650.
CS 16F	45"	French Provincial Brown Oak	3,650.
CS 16I	45"	Italian Provincial Walnut	3,650.
CS 16I	45"	Italian Provincial Cherry	3,650.
CS 16QA	45"	Queen Anne Cherry	3,650.
CS 16QA	45"	Queen Anne Brown Oak	3,650.
US 16ST	45"	Polished Ebony (school)	3,160.
US 16ST	45"	Brown Oak (school)	3,240.
US 16ST	45"	Cherry (school)	3,240.
US 16TC	45"	Polished Ebony	3,120.
US 16TC	45"	Other Finishes	3,240.
CS 19F	47"	French Provincial Brown Oak	3,700.
CS 19F	47"	French Provincial Cherry	3,700.
CS 19M	47"	Mediterranean Brown Oak	3,700.
CS 19M	47"	Mediterranean Cherry	3,700.
US 19T	47"	Polished Ebony	3,200.
US 19T	47"	Cherry	3,240.
US 19T	47"	Other Finishes	3,320.
US 22F	48"	Demi-Chippendale Polished Ebony	3,490.
US 22F	48"	Demi-Chippendale Other Finishes	3,610.
US 22T	48"	Polished Ebony	3,370.
US 22T	48"	Other Finishes	3,490.
US 32T	52"	Polished Ebony	3,620.
US 32T	52"	Other Finishes	3,740.

Grands

Model	Size	Style and Finish	Price*
GS 42	4' 8"	Polished Ebony	8,420.
GS 42	4' 8"	Polished Ivory/White	8,620.
GS 42	4' 8"	Other Finishes	8,820.
GS 52	5'	Polished Ebony	9,260.
GS 52	5'	Polished Ivory/White	9,460.
GS 52	5'	Other Finishes	9,660.
GS 62	5' 4"	Polished Ebony	10,290.

Model	Size	Style and Finish	Price*
GS 62	5' 4"	Polished Ivory/White	10,490.
GS 62	5' 4"	Other Finishes	10,690.
GS 62F	5' 4"	French Provincial Polished Ebony	10,890.
GS 62F	5' 4"	French Provincial Polished Ivory/White	11,090.
GS 62F	5' 4"	French Provincial Cherry	11,090.
GS 62F	5' 4"	French Provincial Brown Oak	11,090.
GS 62F	5' 4"	French Provincial Other Finishes	11,290.
GS 72	5' 8"	Polished Ebony	11,320.
GS 72	5' 8"	Polished Ivory/White	11,520.
GS 72	5' 8"	Other Finishes	11,720.
GS 72F	5' 8"	French Provincial Polished Walnut	12,320.
GS 87	6' 2"	Ebony	12,540.
GS 87	6' 2"	Polished Ebony	12,340.
GS 87	6' 2"	Polished Ivory/White	12,540.
GS 87	6' 2"	Brown Oak	12,540.
GS 87	6' 2"	Brown Mahogany	12,540.
GS 87	6' 2"	Walnut	12,540.
GS 87	6' 2"	Other Finishes	12,740.
GS 87F	6' 2"	French Provincial Mahogany	13,340.
GS 87F	6' 2"	French Provincial Walnut	13,340.

Steinberg, Wilh.

Verticals

Model	Size	Style and Finish	Price
IQ 22	49"	Polished Ebony	12,664.
IQ 22	49"	Mahogany	12,916.
IQ 22	49"	Walnut	12,916.
IQ 22	49"	Oak	12,664.
IQ 22	49"	Cherry	13,470.
IQ 22	49"	Cherry with Yew	14,276.
IQ 22	49"	Beech	12,664.
IQ 22	49"	Alder	12,664.
IQ 22	49"	"Amadeus" Polished Ebony	14,012.
IQ 22	49"	"Amadeus" Mahogany	14,276.
IQ 22	49"	"Amadeus" Walnut	14,276.
IQ 28	52"	Polished Ebony	15,889.
IQ 28	52"	Mahogany	16,015.
IQ 28	52"	Walnut	16,015.
IQ 28	52"	Cherry	16,267.

*For explanation of terms and prices, please see pages 54–60.

Model	Size	Style and Finish	Price*

Steinberg, Wilh. (continued)

IQ 28	52"	Cherry with Yew	16,670.
IQ 28	52"	"Amadeus" Polished Ebony	16,670.
IQ 28	52"	"Amadeus" Cherry	17,048.
IQ 28	52"	"Passione" Polished Ebony	18,082.
IQ 28	52"	"Passione" Mahogany	18,560.
IQ 28	52"	"Passione" Walnut	18,560.
		Inlays, add'l	580.

Grands

IQ 77	5' 9"	Polished Ebony	39,674.
IQ 77	5' 9"	Mahogany	40,808.
IQ 77	5' 9"	Walnut	40,808.
IQ 77	5' 9"	Cherry	41,690.
IQ 77	5' 9"	Pyramid Mahogany with Inlays	43,933.
IQ 99	6' 3"	Polished Ebony	46,100.
IQ 99	6' 3"	Mahogany	51,644.
IQ 99	6' 3"	Walnut	51,644.
IQ 99	6' 3"	Cherry	52,904.
IQ 99	6' 3"	Pyramid Mahogany with Inlays	54,769.

Steingraeber & Söhne

This list includes only those models most likely to be offered to U.S. customers. Other models, styles, and finishes are available.

Verticals

130	51"	Polished Ebony	35,780.
130	51"	Special Veneers	37,840.
138	54"	Polished Ebony	39,550.
138	54"	Polished Ebony with Wood Accents	41,200.
138	54"	"Baroque" Burl Walnut	51,920.

Grands

168N	5' 6"	Polished Ebony	65,950.
168N	5' 6"	Special Veneers	77,140.
168K	5' 6"	"Classicism" Polished Ebony	76,800.
168K	5' 6"	"Classicism" Pol. Ebony w/Pyr. Mahogany	81,900.
168K	5' 6"	"Classicism" Pol. Ebony w/Burl Walnut	81,900.
205N	6' 9"	Polished Ebony	87,800.
205N	6' 9"	Special Veneers	99,800.
205K	6' 9"	"Classicism" Polished Ebony	98,220.

Model	Size	Style and Finish	Price*
205K	6' 9"	"Classicism" Pol. Ebony w/Pyr. Mahogany	105,920.
205K	6' 9"	"Classicism" Pol. Ebony w/Burl Walnut	105,920.
E-272	8' 11"	Polished Ebony	173,800.

Steinway & Sons

Verticals

4510	45"	Sheraton Ebony	19,900.
4510	45"	Sheraton Mahogany	21,900.
4510	45"	Sheraton Walnut	22,600.
4510	45"	Sheraton Dark Cherry	23,300.
4510	45"	Macassar Ebony	28,200.
4510	45"	Marbelized	27,200.
1098	46-1/2"	Ebony	18,900.
1098	46-1/2"	Mahogany	20,200.
1098	46-1/2"	Walnut	21,000.
1098	46-1/2"	Dark Cherry	21,800.
1098	46-1/2"	Marbelized	25,700.
K-52	52"	Ebony	24,700.
K-52	52"	Mahogany	27,800.
K-52	52"	Walnut	28,600.
K-52	52"	East Indian Rosewood	35,700.
K-52	52"	Marbelized	33,300.

Grands

S	5' 1"	Ebony	40,600.
S	5' 1"	Mahogany	45,300.
S	5' 1"	Walnut	46,600.
S	5' 1"	Figured Sapele	49,200.
S	5' 1"	Dark Cherry	49,500.
S	5' 1"	Kewazinga Bubinga	50,600.
S	5' 1"	African Cherry	52,400.
S	5' 1"	Satinwood	55,500.
S	5' 1"	Santos Rosewood	56,400.
S	5' 1"	Pearwood	56,700.
S	5' 1"	East Indian Rosewood	57,400.
S	5' 1"	African Pommele	57,800.
S	5' 1"	Macassar Ebony	63,300.
S	5' 1"	Marbelized	56,400.
S	5' 1"	Hepplewhite Dark Cherry	50,800.

*For explanation of terms and prices, please see pages 54–60.

Model	Size	Style and Finish	Price*

Steinway & Sons (continued)

Model	Size	Style and Finish	Price*
M	5' 7"	Ebony	43,900.
M	5' 7"	Mahogany	49,200.
M	5' 7"	Walnut	50,600.
M	5' 7"	Figured Sapele	52,600.
M	5' 7"	Dark Cherry	53,000.
M	5' 7"	Kewazinga Bubinga	55,200.
M	5' 7"	African Cherry	55,900.
M	5' 7"	Satinwood	59,000.
M	5' 7"	Santos Rosewood	60,700.
M	5' 7"	Pearwood	61,100.
M	5' 7"	East Indian Rosewood	61,700.
M	5' 7"	African Pommele	62,100.
M	5' 7"	Macassar Ebony	67,900.
M	5' 7"	Marbelized	61,400.
M	5' 7"	Hepplewhite Dark Cherry	55,400.
M 1014A	5' 7"	Chippendale Mahogany	60,100.
M 1014A	5' 7"	Chippendale Walnut	61,500.
M 501A	5' 7"	Louis XV Walnut	78,500.
M 501A	5' 7"	Louis XV East Indian Rosewood	91,100.
L	5' 10-1/2"	Ebony	49,000.
L	5' 10-1/2"	Mahogany	55,200.
L	5' 10-1/2"	Walnut	56,400.
L	5' 10-1/2"	Figured Sapele	58,700.
L	5' 10-1/2"	Dark Cherry	59,700.
L	5' 10-1/2"	Kewazinga Bubinga	61,700.
L	5' 10-1/2"	African Cherry	63,000.
L	5' 10-1/2"	Satinwood	64,600.
L	5' 10-1/2"	Santos Rosewood	68,800.
L	5' 10-1/2"	Pearwood	69,200.
L	5' 10-1/2"	East Indian Rosewood	69,800.
L	5' 10-1/2"	African Pommele	70,100.
L	5' 10-1/2"	Macassar Ebony	76,300.
L	5' 10-1/2"	Marbelized	67,900.
L	5' 10-1/2"	Hepplewhite Dark Cherry	62,100.
L	5' 10-1/2"	Limited Edition 150th Historic Ebony	65,000.
L	5' 10-1/2"	Limited Ed. 150th Historic African Cherry	72,800.
L	5' 10-1/2"	Ltd. Ed. 150th Historic East Indian Rosewd.	83,000.
A	6' 2"	Limited Edition Tricentennial Pol. Ebony	75,700.
A	6' 2"	Limited Edition Lagerfield Ebony	85,000.

Model	Size	Style and Finish	Price*
B	6' 10-1/2"	Ebony	62,100.
B	6' 10-1/2"	Mahogany	69,800.
B	6' 10-1/2"	Walnut	71,400.
B	6' 10-1/2"	Figured Sapele	74,600.
B	6' 10-1/2"	Dark Cherry	76,000.
B	6' 10-1/2"	Kewazinga Bubinga	78,100.
B	6' 10-1/2"	African Cherry	78,500.
B	6' 10-1/2"	Satinwood	78,900.
B	6' 10-1/2"	Santos Rosewood	86,800.
B	6' 10-1/2"	Pearwood	87,200.
B	6' 10-1/2"	East Indian Rosewood	88,000.
B	6' 10-1/2"	African Pommele	88,400.
B	6' 10-1/2"	Macassar Ebony	96,100.
B	6' 10-1/2"	Marbelized	82,700.
B	6' 10-1/2"	Hepplewhite Dark Cherry	78,900.
B	6' 10-1/2"	Limited Edition 150th Historic Ebony	86,200.
B	6' 10-1/2"	Limited Ed. 150th Historic African Cherry	96,600.
B	6' 10-1/2"	Ltd. Ed. 150th Historic East Indian Rosewd.	110,200.
D	8' 11-3/4"	Ebony	92,600.
D	8' 11-3/4"	Mahogany	101,400.
D	8' 11-3/4"	Walnut	103,200.
D	8' 11-3/4"	Figured Sapele	107,700.
D	8' 11-3/4"	Dark Cherry	109,700.
D	8' 11-3/4"	Kewazinga Bubinga	112,100.
D	8' 11-3/4"	African Cherry	114,800.
D	8' 11-3/4"	Satinwood	116,800.
D	8' 11-3/4"	Santos Rosewood	124,700.
D	8' 11-3/4"	Pearwood	125,100.
D	8' 11-3/4"	East Indian Rosewood	125,700.
D	8' 11-3/4"	African Pommele	126,000.
D	8' 11-3/4"	Macassar Ebony	137,600.
D	8' 11-3/4"	Hepplewhite Dark Cherry	114,100.

Grands (Hamburg)

I frequently get requests for prices of pianos made in Steinway's branch factory in Hamburg, Germany. Officially, these pianos are not sold in North America, but it is possible to order one through an American Steinway dealer, or to go to Europe and purchase one there. The following list shows approximately how much it would cost to purchase a Hamburg Steinway in Europe and have it shipped to the United States. The list was derived by taking the published retail price in Europe, subtracting the value-added tax not applicable to foreign purchasers, converting to U.S. dollars (the

*For explanation of terms and prices, please see pages 54–60.

Steinway & Sons (continued)

rate used here is 1 Euro = $1.20, but is obviously subject to change), and adding approximate charges for duty, air freight, crating, insurance, brokerage fees, and delivery. Only prices for grands in polished ebony are shown here. *Caution:* This list is published for general informational purposes only. The price that Steinway would charge for a piano ordered through an American Steinway dealer may be different. (Also, the cost of a trip to Europe to purchase the piano is not included!)

Model	Size	Style and Finish	Price
S-155	5' 1"	Polished Ebony	52,200.
M-170	5' 7"	Polished Ebony	57,200.
O-180	5' 10-1/2"	Polished Ebony	61,100.
A-188	6' 2"	Polished Ebony	65,000.
B-211	6' 11"	Polished Ebony	75,200.
C-227	7' 5-1/2"	Polished Ebony	89,200.
D-274	8' 11-3/4"	Polished Ebony	122,200.

Story & Clark

Verticals

Model	Size	Style and Finish	Price
111	45"	Continental Polished Ebony	2,790.
111	45"	Continental Polished Red Mahogany	2,790.
112	45"	"Arlington" Fruitwood	3,990.
112	45"	"Arlington" Cherry	3,990.
113	45"	"Charleston" Fruitwood	3,990.
113	45"	"Charleston" Cherry	3,990.
114	45"	Polished Ebony	3,790.
114	45"	Oak	3,790.
114	45"	Fruitwood	3,790.
115	45"	Queen Anne Polished Ebony	3,190.
115	45"	Queen Anne Polished Red Mahogany	3,190.
115	45"	Queen Anne with QRS CD2000 Player	5,990.
115	45"	Queen Anne with QRS Wireless Player	6,990.
120	47"	Polished Ebony	4,390.
120	47"	Polished Red Mahogany	4,390.
120	47"	Polished Brown Mahogany	4,390.
126	49"	Polished Ebony	3,990.
140	53"	Polished Red Mahogany	6,190.

Grands

Model	Size	Style and Finish	Price
152	5'	Ebony	8,490.
152	5'	Polished Ebony	7,890.
152	5'	Mahogany	8,490.

Model	Size	Style and Finish	Price*
152	5'	Polished Red Mahogany	8,490.
152	5'	Polished Brown Ribbon Mahogany	8,490.
152	5'	Polished Ebony w/ QRS CD2000 Player	11,990.
152	5'	Other Finishes w/QRS CD2000 Player	12,590.
152	5'	Polished Ebony w/QRS Wireless Player	12,990.
152	5'	Other Finishes w/QRS Wireless Player	13,590.
152 I	5'	"Imperial" Polished Ebony	10,290.
152 I	5'	"Imperial" Polished Ebony w/CD2000	14,790.
152 I	5'	"Imperial" Polished Ebony w/Wireless	15,790.
152 S	5'	French Provincial Polished Ebony	9,890.
152 S	5'	French Provincial Pol. Red Mahogany	9,890.
152 S	5'	French Prov. Pol. Brn. Ribbon Mahogany	9,890.
152 S	5'	French Provincial All Finishes w/CD2000	14,390.
152 S	5'	French Provincial All Finishes w/Wireless	15,390.
165	5' 5"	Polished Ebony	9,490.
165	5' 5"	Polished Red Mahogany	10,090.
165	5' 5"	Polished Brown Ribbon Mahogany	10,090.
165	5' 5"	Polished Ebony w/CD2000 Player	13,990.
165	5' 5"	Other Finishes w/CD2000 Player	14,590.
165	5' 5"	Polished Ebony w/Wireless Player	14,990.
165	5' 5"	Other Finishes w/Wireless Player	15,590.
185	6' 1"	Polished Ebony	11,890.
185	6' 1"	Polished Red Mahogany	12,490.
185	6' 1"	Polished Brown Ribbon Mahogany	12,490.
185	6' 1"	Polished Ebony w/CD2000 Player	15,990.
185	6' 1"	Other Finishes w/CD2000 Player	16,590.
185	6' 1"	Polished Ebony w/Wireless Player	16,990.
185	6' 1"	Other Finishes w/Wireless Player	17,590.

Suzuki

Verticals

Model	Size	Style and Finish	Price*
AU-100	44-1/2"	Continental Polished Ebony	2,498.
AU-100	44-1/2"	Continental Polished Red Mahogany	2,498.
AU-200	46"	Polished Ebony	2,798.
AU-200	46"	Polished Red Mahogany	2,798.
AU-210	46"	French Provincial Polished Ebony	2,998.
AU-210	46"	French Provincial Red Mahogany	3,198.
AU-210	46"	French Provincial Polished Red Mahogany	2,998.

*For explanation of terms and prices, please see pages 54–60.

Model	Size	Style and Finish	Price*

Suzuki (continued)

Model	Size	Style and Finish	Price*
AU-210	46"	French Provincial Oak	3,198.
AU-300	48-1/2"	Polished Ebony	2,998.
AU-300	48-1/2"	Polished Red Mahogany	2,998.
AU-310	48-1/2"	"European Ornate" Polished Ebony	3,198.
AU-310	48-1/2"	"European Ornate" Red Mahogany	3,398.
AU-310	48-1/2"	"European Ornate" Polished Red Mahogany	3,198.
AU-310	48-1/2"	"European Ornate" Oak	3,398.

Grands

Model	Size	Style and Finish	Price*
AG-500	5'	Polished Ebony	7,980.
AG-500	5'	Polished Brown Mahogany	8,380.
AG-500	5'	Polished Red Mahogany	8,380.
AG-550	5' 5"	Polished Ebony	8,980.
AG-550	5' 5"	Polished Brown Mahogany	9,380.
AG-550	5' 5"	Polished Red Mahogany	9,380.
AG-600	6'	Polished Ebony	11,580.

Vogel

Verticals

Model	Size	Style and Finish	Price*
V-115 M	45"	Continental Polished Ebony	9,780.
V-115 M	45"	Continental Wood Finish	9,180.
V-115 T	45"	Polished Ebony	9,780.

Grands

Model	Size	Style and Finish	Price*
V-177 CH	5' 10"	Chippendale Polished Ebony	26,180.
V-177 CH	5' 10"	Chippendale Polished Mahogany	27,380.
V-177 CH	5' 10"	Chippendale Polished Walnut	27,380.
V-177 R	5' 10"	"Royal" Polished Ebony	26,180.
V-177 R	5' 10"	"Royal" Polished Mahogany	27,380.
V-177 R	5' 10"	"Royal" Polished Walnut	27,380.
V-177 RI	5' 10"	"Royal" Polished Mahogany Intarsia	29,580.
V-177 RI	5' 10"	"Royal" Polished Flame Mahogany Coffer	29,580.
V-177 T	5' 10"	Polished Ebony	22,980.
V-177 T	5' 10"	Polished Mahogany	24,180.
V-177 T	5' 10"	Polished Walnut	24,180.
V-177 TI	5' 10"	Polished Mahogany Intarsia	31,380.

Model	Size	Style and Finish	Price*

Walter, Charles R.

Verticals

Model	Size	Style and Finish	Price
1520	43"	Oak	7,810.
1520	43"	Cherry	8,080.
1520	43"	Walnut	8,100.
1520	43"	Mahogany	8,240.
1520	43"	Riviera Oak	7,790.
1520	43"	Italian Provincial Oak	7,820.
1520	43"	Italian Provincial Walnut	8,120.
1520	43"	Italian Provincial Mahogany	8,260.
1520	43"	French Provincial Oak	8,120.
1520	43"	French Provincial Walnut	8,360.
1520	43"	French Provincial Mahogany	8,360.
1520	43"	French Provincial Cherry	8,360.
1520	43"	Country Classic Oak	7,860.
1520	43"	Country Classic Cherry	8,010.
1520	43"	Queen Anne Oak	8,180.
1520	43"	Queen Anne Cherry	8,360.
1520	43"	Queen Anne Mahogany	8,360.
1500	45"	Ebony	7,580.
1500	45"	Semi-Gloss Ebony	7,680.
1500	45"	Polished Ebony	7,780.
1500	45"	Oak	7,180.
1500	45"	Walnut	7,520.
1500	45"	Mahogany	7,730.
1500	45"	Cherry	7,710.
1500	45"	Gothic Oak	7,710.

Grands

Model	Size	Style and Finish	Price
W-190	6' 4"	Ebony	33,580.
W-190	6' 4"	Semi-Polished and Polished Ebony	34,440.
W-190	6' 4"	Mahogany	35,070.
W-190	6' 4"	Semi-Polished and Polished Mahogany	35,950.
W-190	6' 4"	Walnut	35,070.
W-190	6' 4"	Open-Pore Walnut	34,230.
W-190	6' 4"	Semi-Polished and Polished Walnut	35,950.
W-190	6' 4"	Cherry	35,070.
W-190	6' 4"	Semi-Polished and Polished Cherry	35,950.
W-190	6' 4"	Oak	32,290.
W-190	6' 4"	Chippendale Mahogany	36,160.

*For explanation of terms and prices, please see pages 54–60.

Model	Size	Style and Finish	Price*

Walter, Charles R. (continued)

Model	Size	Style and Finish	Price*
W-190	6' 4"	Chippendale Semi-Pol. and Pol. Mahogany	37,020.
W-190	6' 4"	Chippendale Cherry	36,160.
W-190	6' 4"	Chippendale Semi-Pol. and Polished Cherry	37,020.

Weinbach

Note: Prices below do not include bench. Add from $220 to $630 (most are under $400), depending on choice of bench.

Verticals

Model	Size	Style and Finish	Price
114-I	45"	Demi-Chippendale Polished Ebony	6,180.
114-I	45"	Demi-Chippendale Polished Walnut	6,180.
114-I	45"	Demi-Chippendale Polished Mahogany	6,180.
114-IC	45"	Chippendale Polished Ebony	6,500.
114-IC	45"	Chippendale Polished Walnut	6,500.
114-IC	45"	Chippendale Polished Mahogany	6,500.
114-II	45"	Polished Ebony	5,500.
114-IV	45"	Polished Ebony	5,900.
114-IV	45"	Polished Walnut	5,900.
114-IV	45"	Polished Mahogany	5,900.
124-III	50"	Polished Ebony	7,100.
124-III	50"	Polished Walnut	7,100.
124-III	50"	Polished Mahogany	7,100.

Grands

Model	Size	Style and Finish	Price
155	5' 3"	Polished Ebony	18,780.
155	5' 3"	Polished Walnut	18,780.
155	5' 3"	Polished Mahogany	18,780.
170	5' 8"	Polished Ebony	19,800.
170	5' 8"	Polished Walnut	19,800.
170	5' 8"	Polished Mahogany	19,800.
170 C	5' 8"	Chippendale Polished Walnut	23,800.
170 C	5' 8"	Chippendale Polished Mahogany	23,800.
192	6' 4"	Polished Ebony	23,000.
192	6' 4"	Polished Walnut	23,000.
192	6' 4"	Polished Mahogany	23,000.

Model	Size	Style and Finish	Price*

Wurlitzer

Grands

Model	Size	Style and Finish	Price*
C143	4' 7"	Polished Mahogany	9,298.
C143	4' 7"	Polished Oak	9,298.
C143	4' 7"	Polished White	9,028.
C153	5' 1"	Ebony and Polished Ebony	10,440.
C153	5' 1"	Polished Mahogany	10,800.
C153	5' 1"	Oak	10,800.
C153	5' 1"	Walnut	10,800.
C153	5' 1"	Polished Ivory	10,440.
C153QA	5' 1"	Queen Anne Polished Mahogany	12,600.
C153QA	5' 1"	Queen Anne Oak	12,600.
C153QA	5' 1"	Queen Anne Cherry	12,600.
C173	5' 8"	Ebony and Polished Ebony	11,520.
C173	5' 8"	Polished Mahogany	11,872.
C173	5' 8"	Polished White	11,520.
WP153	5' 1"	Ebony	11,580.
WP153	5' 1"	Polished Ebony	10,990.
WP153	5' 1"	Polished Mahogany	11,580.
WP173	5' 8"	Ebony	12,990.
WP173	5' 8"	Polished Ebony	12,390.
WP173	5' 8"	Polished Mahogany	12,990.

Wyman

Verticals

Model	Size	Style and Finish	Price*
WV96	37"	American Country Gallery Oak	2,790.
WV96	37"	French Provincial Sable Cherry	2,850.
WV99	39"	Continental Polished Ebony (73)	1,798.
WV99	39"	Continental Polished Cherry (73)	1,898.
WV108	42-1/2"	Continental Polished Ebony	2,550.
WV108	42-1/2"	Continental Polished Mahogany	2,590.
WV108	42-1/2"	Continental Polished Cherry	2,590.
WV110	43"	American Country Gallery Oak	2,970.
WV110	43"	Sable Brown Mahogany	2,970.
WV110	43"	French Provincial Sable Cherry	3,050.
WV110	43"	Country French Oak	3,050.
WV117	46"	Polished Ebony	2,900.
WV120	48"	Polished Ebony (straight legs)	3,150.
WV120	48"	Polished Mahogany (curved legs)	3,190.

*For explanation of terms and prices, please see pages 54–60.

Model	Size	Style and Finish	Price*

Wyman (continued)

Grands

Model	Size	Style and Finish	Price*
WG145	4' 9"	Ebony	7,990.
WG145	4' 9"	Polished Ebony	7,390.
WG145	4' 9"	Mahogany and Polished Mahogany	7,990.
WG145	4' 9"	Cherry and Polished Cherry	7,990.
WG145	4' 9"	Polished Snow White	7,990.
WG150	4' 11"	Ebony	8,390.
WG150	4' 11"	Polished Ebony	7,790.
WG150	4' 11"	Mahogany and Polished Mahogany	8,390.
WG150	4' 11"	Cherry and Polished Cherry	8,390.
WG150	4' 11"	Polished Snow White	8,390.
WG160	5' 3"	Ebony	8,790.
WG160	5' 3"	Polished Ebony	8,390.
WG160	5' 3"	Mahogany and Polished Mahogany	8,790.
WG160	5' 3"	Cherry and Polished Cherry	8,790.
WG160	5' 3"	Polished Snow White	8,790.
WG170	5' 7"	Ebony	9,390.
WG170	5' 7"	Polished Ebony	8,990.
WG170	5' 7"	Mahogany and Polished Mahogany	9,390.
WG170	5' 7"	Cherry and Polished Cherry	9,390.
WG170	5' 7"	Polished Snow White	9,390.
All Grands		Round or Curved Legs, any finish, add'l	200.

Yamaha

Verticals

Model	Size	Style and Finish	Price*
M112	44"	Continental Ebony	5,090.
M112	44"	Continental Polished Ebony	5,190.
M112	44"	Continental American Walnut	5,290.
M112	44"	Continental Polished Mahogany	6,390.
M112	44"	Continental Polished Ivory/White	6,290.
M450	44"	Cherry	3,790.
M450	44"	Brown Cherry	3,790.
M475	44"	Mahogany	4,290.
M475	44"	Italian Provincial Cherry	4,290.
M500	44"	Chippendale Brown Mahogany	5,990.
M500	44"	Florentine Light Oak	4,890.
M500	44"	Georgian Mahogany	5,990.
M500	44"	Hancock Brown Cherry	4,290.

Model	Size	Style and Finish	Price*
M500	44"	Milano Dark Oak	4,890.
M500	44"	Parisian Cherry and Dark Cherry	6,190.
M500	44"	Queen Anne Cherry and Dark Cherry	5,090.
M500	44"	Sheraton Mahogany	4,290.
P22	45"	American Walnut	5,190.
P22	45"	Black, Dark, or Light Oak	5,190.
T116	45"	Polished Ebony	5,390.
T116	45"	Polished Mahogany	6,390.
P600	45"	Sheraton Brown Mahogany	5,990.
P600	45"	Queen Anne Brown Cherry	5,990.
P600	45"	Tuscan Ash	6,190.
T121	48"	Polished Ebony	6,390.
U1	48"	Ebony	8,190.
U1	48"	Polished Ebony	7,990.
U1	48"	American Walnut	8,700.
U1	48"	Polished American Walnut	9,300.
U1	48"	Polished Mahogany	9,300.
U1	48"	Polished White	9,390.
U3	52"	Polished Ebony	10,690.
U3	52"	Polished Mahogany	12,390.
U5	52"	Polished Ebony	12,990.
U5	52"	Polished Mahogany	15,390.

Disklavier Verticals

Model	Size	Style and Finish	Price*
MX500	44"	Chippendale Brown Mahogany	10,990.
MX500	44"	Florentine Light Oak	9,790
MX500	44"	Georgian Mahogany	10,790.
MX500	44"	Milano Dark Oak	9,790.
MX500	44"	Parisian Cherry and Dark Cherry	10,990.
MX500	44"	Queen Anne Cherry and Dark Cherry	9,990.
MX22	45"	American Walnut	10,190.
MX22	45"	Dark, Black, and Light Oak	10,190.
MX116	45"	Polished Ebony	10,390.
MX116	45"	Polished Mahogany	11,390
MX600	45"	Sheraton Brown Mahogany	10,990.
MX600	45"	Queen Anne Dark Cherry	10,990.
MX600	45"	Tuscan Ash	11,190.

MIDIPiano (Silent) Verticals

Model	Size	Style and Finish	Price*
MP500	44"	Cottage Cherry	7,590.
MP500	44"	Florentine Light Oak	7,590.

*For explanation of terms and prices, please see pages 54–60.

153

Model	Size	Style and Finish	Price*

Yamaha (continued)

Model	Size	Style and Finish	Price*
MP500	44"	Georgian Mahogany	8,590.
MP500	44"	Hancock Brown Cherry	7,090.
MP500	44"	Milano Dark Oak	7,590.
MP500	44"	Parisian Cherry	8,790.
MP500	44"	Queen Anne Cherry and Dark Cherry	7,790.
MP500	44"	Sheraton Mahogany	7,090.
MP22	45"	American Walnut	7,790.
MPU1	48"	Polished Ebony	10,790.

Disklavier Verticals with Silent Feature

Model	Size	Style and Finish	Price*
DU1A	48"	Polished Ebony	15,790.
DU1A	48"	American Walnut	16,390.
DU1A	48"	Polished Mahogany	17,090.
DU1A	48"	Polished White	17,190.

Grands

Model	Size	Style and Finish	Price*
GA1E	4' 11"	Polished Ebony	9,990.
GC1	5' 3"	Ebony	15,590.
GC1	5' 3"	Polished Ebony	15,390.
GC1	5' 3"	American Walnut	16,990.
GC1	5' 3"	Polished American Walnut	16,990.
GC1	5' 3"	Polished Mahogany	16,990.
GC1	5' 3"	Polished Ivory/White	16,590.
GC1FP	5' 3"	French Provincial Brown Cherry	17,990.
GC1G	5' 3"	Georgian Brown Mahogany	17,990.
C1	5' 3"	Ebony	20,190.
C1	5' 3"	Polished Ebony	19,990.
C1	5' 3"	American Walnut	22,390.
C1	5' 3"	Polished American Walnut	23,390.
C1	5' 3"	Mahogany and Polished Mahogany	23,390.
C1	5' 3"	Polished White	22,390.
C1	5' 3"	"Metro" Polished Ebony and Gold	24,590.
C2	5' 8"	Ebony	22,790.
C2	5' 8"	Polished Ebony	22,590.
C2	5' 8"	American Walnut	25,590.
C2	5' 8"	Polished American Walnut	26,390.
C2	5' 8"	Polished Mahogany	26,390.
C2	5' 8"	Light American Oak	25,590.
C2	5' 8"	Polished White	24,390.
C3	6' 1"	Ebony	31,190.

Model	Size	Style and Finish	Price*
C3	6' 1"	Polished Ebony	30,790.
C3	6' 1"	American Walnut	33,790.
C3	6' 1"	Polished Mahogany	35,590.
C3	6' 1"	Polished White	34,390.
S4	6' 3"	Polished Ebony	54,990.
C5	6' 7"	Ebony	33,590.
C5	6' 7"	Polished Ebony	33,190.
C5	6' 7"	Polished Mahogany	42,190.
C6	6' 11"	Ebony	37,390.
C6	6' 11"	Polished Ebony	36,790.
C6	6' 11"	Polished Mahogany	44,190.
S6	6' 11"	Polished Ebony	62,390.
C7	7' 6"	Ebony	42,190.
C7	7' 6"	Polished Ebony	42,190.
C7	7' 6"	Polished Mahogany	48,390.
CFIIIS	9'	Polished Ebony	113,790.

Disklavier Grands

Model	Size	Style and Finish	Price*
DGA1E	4' 11"	Polished Ebony (playback only)	17,590.
DGC1	5' 3"	Polished Ebony (playback only)	23,390.
DGC1A	5' 3"	Ebony	29,230.
DGC1A	5' 3"	Polished Ebony	29,030.
DGC1A	5' 3"	American Walnut	30,630.
DGC1A	5' 3"	Polished American Walnut	30,630.
DGC1A	5' 3"	Mahogany and Polished Mahogany	30,630.
DGC1A	5' 3"	Polished Ivory/White	30,230.
DC1A	5' 3"	Ebony	33,830.
DC1A	5' 3"	Polished Ebony	33,630.
DC1A	5' 3"	American Walnut	36,030.
DC1A	5' 3"	Polished American Walnut	37,030.
DC1A	5' 3"	Mahogany and Polished Mahogany	37,030.
DC1A	5' 3"	Polished Ivory/White	36,030.
DC1A	5' 3"	"Metro" Polished Ebony and Gold	38,230.
DC2A	5' 8"	Ebony	36,430.
DC2A	5' 8"	Polished Ebony	36,230.
DC2A	5' 8"	American Walnut	39,230.
DC2A	5' 8"	Polished American Walnut	40,030.
DC2A	5' 8"	Polished Mahogany	40,030.
DC2A	5' 8"	Polished Light American Oak	40,030.
DC2A	5' 8"	Polished White	38,030.

*For explanation of terms and prices, please see pages 54–60.

Model	Size	Style and Finish	Price*

Yamaha (continued)

Model	Size	Style and Finish	Price*
DC3A	6' 1"	Ebony	45,430.
DC3A	6' 1"	Polished Ebony	45,030.
DC3A	6' 1"	American Walnut	48,030.
DC3A	6' 1"	Polished Mahogany	49,830.
DC3A	6' 1"	Polished White	
DC5A	6' 7"	Ebony	47,830.
DC5A	6' 7"	Polished Ebony	47,430.
DC5A	6' 7"	Polished Mahogany	56,430.
DC6A	6' 11"	Ebony	51,630.
DC6A	6' 11"	Polished Ebony	51,030.
DC6A	6' 11"	Polished Mahogany	62,530.
DC7A	7' 6"	Ebony	56,830.
DC7A	7' 6"	Polished Ebony	56,430.

Disklavier Pro Grands

Model	Size	Style and Finish	Price*
DC3APRO	6' 1"	Polished Ebony	52,990.
DS4APRO	6' 3"	Polished Ebony	79,390.
DC5APRO	6' 7"	Polished Ebony	55,390.
DC6APRO	6' 11"	Polished Ebony	58,990.
DS6APRO	6' 11"	Polished Ebony	86,790.
DC7APRO	7' 6"	Polished Ebony	66,190.
DCFIIISAPRO	9'	Polished Ebony	143,100.

MIDIPiano (Silent) Grands

Model	Size	Style and Finish	Price*
MPC1	5' 3"	Polished Ebony	25,190.
MPC2	5' 8"	Polished Ebony	27,790.
MPC3	6' 1"	Polished Ebony	35,890.
MPC6	6' 11"	Polished Ebony	41,990.
MPC7	7' 6"	Polished Ebony	47,290.

Young Chang

See also under "Bergmann" and "Pramberger."

Verticals

Model	Size	Style and Finish	Price*
GE-102	43"	Continental Polished Ebony	3,590.
GE-102	43"	Continental Polished Red Mahogany	3,700.
GE-102	43"	Continental Polished Brown Mahogany	3,700.
GE-102	43"	Continental Polished Ivory	3,590.
GF-110	43-1/2"	Mahogany	4,440.
GF-110	43-1/2"	Queen Anne Oak	4,440.

Model	Size	Style and Finish	Price*
GF-110	43-1/2"	Mediterranean Oak	4,440.
GF-110	43-1/2"	Queen Anne Cherry	4,440.
GF-110	43-1/2"	French Provincial Cherry	4,440.
PF-110	43-1/2"	Mahogany	5,790.
PF-110	43-1/2"	Queen Anne Oak	5,790.
PF-110	43-1/2"	Mediterranean Oak	5,790.
PF-110	43-1/2"	Queen Anne Cherry	5,790.
PF-110	43-1/2"	French Provincial Cherry	5,790.
GE-116	46-1/2"	Polished Ebony	3,950.
GE-116	46-1/2"	Polished Red Mahogany	4,080.
PF-116	46-1/2"	Mahogany	6,080.
PF-116	46-1/2"	Mediterranean Oak	6,080.
PF-116	46-1/2"	French Provincial Cherry	6,290.
PE-116S	46-1/2"	Ebony	5,390.
PE-116S	46-1/2"	American Walnut	5,590.
PE-116S	46-1/2"	American Oak	5,590.
PE-116S	46-1/2"	American Cherry	5,790.
PE-118	47"	Ebony and Polished Ebony	5,190.
PE-118	47"	Polished Red Mahogany	5,390.
PE-118	47"	Polished Brown Mahogany	5,390.
GE-121	48"	Polished Ebony	4,190.
GE-121	48"	Polished Red Mahogany	4,320.
GE-121	48"	Polished Bubinga	4,520.
PE-121	48"	Ebony and Polished Ebony	5,390.
PE-121	48"	Polished Red Mahogany	5,590.
PE-121	48"	Brown Mahogany	6,390.
PE-121	48"	Polished Brown Mahogany	5,590.
GE-131	52"	Polished Ebony	4,440.
GE-131	52"	Polished Red Mahogany	4,570.
PE-131	52"	Ebony and Polished Ebony	6,290.

Grands

Model	Size	Style and Finish	Price*
GS-150	4' 11-1/2"	Polished Ebony	10,390.
GS-150	4' 11-1/2"	Polished Red Mahogany	10,600.
GS-150	4' 11-1/2"	Polished Walnut	10,600.
GS-150	4' 11-1/2"	Polished Ivory	10,390.
PG-150	4' 11-1/2"	Ebony and Polished Ebony	12,590.
PG-150	4' 11-1/2"	Polished Red Mahogany	13,220.
PG-150	4' 11-1/2"	Polished Brown Mahogany	13,220.
PG-150	4' 11-1/2"	Cherry	13,430.
PG-150	4' 11-1/2"	Polished Ivory/White	13,010.

*For explanation of terms and prices, please see pages 54–60.

Model	Size	Style and Finish	Price*
Young Chang (continued)			
PG-150D	4' 11-1/2"	Queen Anne Polished Mahogany	15,530.
PG-150D	4' 11-1/2"	Queen Anne Cherry	15,740.
PG-150D	4' 11-1/2"	Queen Anne Polished Ivory	15,320.
GS-157	5' 2"	Polished Ebony	11,600.
GS-157	5' 2"	Polished Red Mahogany	11,820.
GS-157	5' 2"	Polished Walnut	11,820.
GS-157	5' 2"	Polished Ivory	11,600.
PG-157	5' 2"	Ebony and Polished Ebony	14,180.
PG-157	5' 2"	Polished Red Mahogany	14,600.
PG-157	5' 2"	Polished Brown Mahogany	14,600.
PG-157	5' 2"	Cherry	14,810.
PG-157	5' 2"	Polished Ivory/White	14,390.
PG-157D	5' 2"	Country French Cherry	17,630.
PG-157D	5' 2"	Queen Anne Mahogany	17,420.
PG-157D	5' 2"	Queen Anne Cherry	17,630.
PG-157D	5' 2"	Empire Polished Brown Mahogany	18,260.
GS-175	5' 9"	Polished Ebony	13,080.
GS-175	5' 9"	Polished Red Mahogany	13,300.
GS-175	5' 9"	Polished Walnut	13,300.
PG-175	5' 9"	Ebony and Polished Ebony	16,160.
PG-175	5' 9"	Polished Red Mahogany	16,790.
PG-175	5' 9"	Polished Brown Mahogany	16,790.
PG-175	5' 9"	Walnut	16,790.
PG-175	5' 9"	Cherry	16,790.
PG-175D	5' 9"	Empire Polished Brown Mahogany	20,360.
GS-185	6' 1"	Polished Ebony	14,080.
GS-185	6' 1"	Polished Red Mahogany	14,280.
GS-185	6' 1"	Polished Walnut	14,280.
PG-185	6' 1"	Ebony and Polished Ebony	18,470.
PG-185	6' 1"	Walnut and Polished Walnut	19,430.
PG-185	6' 1"	Polished Red Mahogany	19,430.
PG-185	6' 1"	Polished Brown Mahogany	19,430.
PG-185	6' 1"	Polished Ivory	19,220.

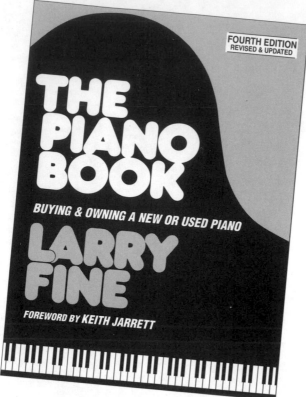

244 pages
8-1/2 x 11
100 line drawings

Paperback $19.95
Shipping/handling $5.00

- *Candid brand-by-brand reviews of new pianos*

- *Sales gimmicks to watch out for—and the real differences in piano quality and features*

- *How to negotiate the best deal*

- *Tips on finding, inspecting, appraising, and buying a used piano*

- *Special section on buying an older Steinway*

- *Piano moving, storage, tuning, servicing*